Creating Websites That Work

Kathryn Summers
University of Baltimore

Michael Summers
User Experience Specialist, Nielson Norman Group

HOUGHTON MIFFLIN COMPANY
Boston   New York

Publisher: Patricia A. Coryell
Executive Editor: Suzanne Phelps Weir
Sponsoring Editor: Michael Gillespie
Associate Editor: Bruce Cantley
Editorial Assistant: Lisa Littlewood
Associate Project Editor: Reba Libby
Editorial Assistant: Rachel Zanders
Senior Production/Design Coordinator: Jodi O'Rourke
Senior Manufacturing Coordinator: Marie Barnes
Marketing Manager: Cindy Graff Cohen

Cover Photography: © Getty Images

Credits are on p. 181, which constitutes an extension of the copyright page.

Printed in the U.S.A.

Library of Congress Catalog Card Number: 2001133356

ISBN: 0-618-22605-2

1 2 3 4 5 6 7 8 9 QUE 08 07 06 05 04

Contents

Preface   vii

1 Creating a Portfolio Site   1

The Web Design Process—Creating an Online Portfolio   2
  Requirements Gathering for a Portfolio Website   2
  Possible Content Items for an Online Portfolio   3

Experience Design   4
  Creating a Portfolio Site Map   5
  Wireframes   6
  Visual Design   8
  Effective Portfolio Content   11

Usability Testing   12
Ethics and Credibility   14
Looking Ahead   15

2 Requirements Gathering   19

Site Owner Business Goals   21
  How Do We Make Money?   21
  What Is the Size of the Market Opportunity?   21
  Who Are the Site's Most Formidable Competitors?   22
  What Are the Specific Revenue and Growth Goals? How Will You Measure Success?   22
  What User Behaviors Best Support the Site Owners' Business Goals?   23

Site Owner Brand Positioning   23
  Who Are the Site Owners' Current Customers or Audience? The Site Owners' Potential Customers?   24
  What Uniquely Ownable Benefit Does or Could the Site Owners' Brand Possess?   25
  What Tone and Image Do Site Owners Want Their Brand to Represent to Their Audience?   26

User Goals   26

Observe Representative Users in Their Environment   29
Debrief and Capture Findings—the Same Day   33
Work in Cross-Functional Teams   33
Confirm Your Hypotheses with Quantitative Research   35

Technical and Human Resources and Requirements   35

Technical Requirements   36
Human Requirements   37

3   Experience Design   40

Making Sense of Your User Data   40

Personas   41
Task Flows   47

Experience Design   49

Creating the Information Architecture and the Site Map   50
Wireframes   58
Visual Designs   61

4   Elements of Effective Visual Design   66

Defining an Overall Look and Feel   67

Consistency   69
Simplicity   69

Creating Page Designs   70

Showing Relationships, Guiding Users Through the Site   72
Visual Grouping—Gestalt Principles   72
Designing Content Elements   80
Layout   88
Evaluating the Success of Your Design   93
Designing the Homepage   94

Capturing Design Decisions in a Style Guide   96

Getting Ready to Test   97

5 Creating Effective Content for the Web   101

Understanding How People Read on the Web   102

Gathering Content Information   103

Keeping Your Content User-Focused   103
Building a Relationship with Users   106
Breaking Content into User-Focused Chunks   107

Structuring Content Visually   108
Keep Your Text Focused and Concise   110
Start Content Chunks with Clear Main Points   112
Use Strong Verbs and the Active Voice   112
Use Lists   112
Use Meaningful Headings and Subheadings   113
Highlight Key Information   114

Making the Most of Your Online Environment   115
Add Links to Further Information   117
Use Scrolling Appropriately   118
Use Frames Cautiously, When Appropriate   119
Include Informational Images and Graphics   120
Use Multimedia Appropriately   120
Use Interactivity Appropriately   123
Make Content Easy to Find   124

Establishing Credibility   125

Keeping Your Communication Ethical   126

Editing Your Content   128

Testing Your Content for Effectiveness   128

6 Usability Analysis   132

What Is a Usability Test?   133
Definition of Usability   133
Using Simplified Usability Test Methods   137

The Usability-Testing Process   139
Developing the Test Plan   140
Selecting and Recruiting Test Participants   145
*Preparing the Test Materials and Setting Up the Testing
    Environment*   149

Conducting the Test   151

Transforming Data into Findings and Recommendations   155

Presenting Results   160

Video Summary of Findings   161

Ethical Video Editing   162

Glossary   167

Index   169

Credits   181

Preface

No matter what your career path—technical communicator, engineer, health services professional, or any other technical professional—you are likely to work with the Web. The Web has become so pervasive, so central to the way organizations work, that it is almost impossible to avoid. How did the architects who designed the new World Trade Center memorial publish their work? The Web. How do nurses who do outpatient care track medical records? The Web. And how do engineers and scientists collaborate with colleagues around the world? Right again—the Web.

Whether or not you have primary design responsibilities for a website, at some point in your career you will produce materials that will be bound for your organization's website, be it an internal "intranet" or the public-facing "internet." It's not enough just to have strong writing skills anymore. You have to know how to produce effective content for the Web—a medium where the rules are different.

The primary goal of this book is to help you, as a technical communicator, design and present information effectively online. We focus on:

- requirements gathering—figuring out what content and functionality need to be available on the site,
- experience design—presenting your content and functionality in a way that creates a unified and enjoyable experience for users, and
- usability—making sure users can find and use your content and functionality effectively.

Effective requirements gathering, experience design, and usability are the keys to building a site that *works*—a site that effectively meets the needs of both the site's owners and its users. Although some may see the Web as the domain of programmers and graphic artists, the truth is that the usefulness of a site's content is a deciding factor in its ongoing appeal. Information design and Web writing make the difference between effective websites and ineffective ones.

Skilled technical communicators obviously have much to offer this field. Creating simple websites is easily within the reach of most technical writing instructors and students, despite any lack of prior experience. We assume that you are already a fairly comfortable and savvy Web consumer, but we do not assume that you have any prior experience creating websites. The activities described in this text are achievable even if you have never designed for the Web. They are connected at every step with general principles of good communication, technical writing, and information design. The principles that you will learn and practice in this course are widely applicable and will continue to be useful even in the most complex, professional projects.

 ## About this Book

This book is about the design process for building effective websites. We combine principles of information design, audience analysis, visual communication, and usability testing with a real-world context of examples drawn from professional practice.

Organization

You'll get a hands-on introduction to these principles and techniques in Chapter 1, "Creating a Portfolio Site." Chapters 2 through 6 explore effective site design methods in more depth as you create a small website for a company or not-for-profit organization. Chapter 2, "Requirements Gathering," helps you identify the business goals, branding goals, user goals, and resources that need to be considered in the site design. Chapter 3, "Experience Design," helps you use site maps, task flows, user descriptions called personas, and prototype sketches called wireframes that help you design the information architecture and user experience. Chapter 4, "Elements of Effective Visual Design," focuses on such topics as relationship of elements, visual grouping, and layout to create the visual look and feel of the site. Chapter 5, "Creating Effective Content for the Web," highlights how to produce and refine content in a Web-appropriate manner. Chapter 6, "Usability Analysis," takes you step-by-step through the testing process to evaluate the usability of your site.

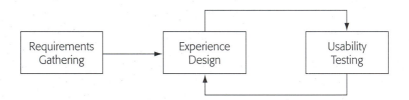

Special Features

- *Numerous illustrations and screen captures throughout the book, including a full-color section,* provide an essential visual component to the book.
- *End-of-chapter Final Checklists* offer handy step-by-step quick references to the website creation process.
- *Professional Profiles* bring a "real world" component to the book by profiling working Web professionals who specialize in areas discussed in the book, such as user design, visual design, and usability.

Accompanying Website

The website for the book includes a wide range of sample materials, so you will have concrete examples of what these tools look like. These sample materials demonstrate the cycle of gathering information, planning, creating prototypes, testing for usability, re-designing, testing again, and planning for future expansion or revision. As you work through the chapters of this text, you will create a website that effectively balances site owner needs and user goals within the constraints of your technical abilities and resources.

Acknowledgements

We would like to thank our editors, Michael Gillespie, Bruce Cantley, and Reba Libby, for supporting us through thick and thin. We'd also like to thank our significant others, Elisa Chang and John Friese, for the many, many missed weekends and altered plans that finishing this book made necessary. ;)

We want to thank our friends and colleagues Alan Cooper, Kara Pernice Coyne, Shelley Evenson, Shannon Ford, Mitchell Gass, Hoa Loranger, Larry Marine, Jakob Nielsen, Janice Redish, Jeffrey Rubin, Thomas Sherman, and Catherine Wilson, for sharing their case studies and life's work with us.

And many thanks to our reviewers, who read the manuscript at various stages of development and whose commentary has significantly helped shape the final book: Valentina Abordonado, Hawaii Pacific University; C. N. Bean, Virginia Tech; Susheel Bibbs, University of California at Berkeley; Elizabeth Ann Cain, Texas A&M University; Ellen Grabiner, Simmons College; Byron Hawk, George Mason University; Jeanne Linsdell, San Jose State University; Wilson Lowrey, Mississippi State University; Michael McCord, University of Nevada–Las Vegas; Roland Nord, Minnesota State University–Mankato; Celia Patterson, Pittsburg State University; Ginger Rosenkrans, Pepperdine University; Patrick M. Scanlon, Rochester Institute of Technology; and Diana Birge Wendt, University of Nebraska at Omaha.

About the Authors:

Kathryn Summers (Ph.D., Texas Christian University) is an assistant professor in the School of Information Arts and Technologies at the University of Baltimore. She teaches user research, information design, technical communication, and rhetorical approaches to information systems, and consults with industry.

Michael Summers (M.S., Syracuse University) is User Experience Specialist at Nielsen Norman Group. Prior to joining NN/g, Michael was Director of User Research at Scient, and Senior Information Architect at USWeb/CKS. His consulting work has included REUTERS, Pfizer, the United States Treasury, Major League Baseball, McNeil, Morgan Stanley, and AltaVista.

1 Creating a Portfolio Site

CHAPTER HIGHLIGHTS

The Web Design Process—Creating an
Online Portfolio
> Requirements Gathering for a Portfolio Website
>> Portfolio Site Owner Goals
>> Portfolio Site User Goals
>> Human and Technical Resources
> Possible Content Items for an Online Portfolio

Experience Design
> Creating a Portfolio Site Map
> Wireframes
> Visual Design
> Effective Portfolio Content

Usability Testing
Ethics and Credibility
Looking Ahead

Some websites are great. They save us time, amuse us, or they give us better access to things that we want. Saving hours in line at the Motor Vehicles Department by renewing a registration on the Web is pretty nice. And we are always impressed by how intuitively we can navigate the BBC's website and come away with a thorough sense of world news.

But if you've spent any time using the Web, you've probably run into sites that are pretty awful. Maybe you've tried to modify your course schedule or attempted to pay your bills online, and you've run into problems because the site was structured like a maze and you couldn't find what you needed.

The question becomes, what does "good" mean when we're talking about websites? And more important, how do you build a good website?

This chapter introduces the Web design process, which we will spend the rest of the book describing in more detail. The best way to learn how to build effective websites is to start with some hands-on experience. Principles and methods are very important, but they won't seem as abstract after you've built something.

1

So we'll begin with a small but important Web project—a professional portfolio site you can use to get a job.

The Web Design Process—Creating an Online Portfolio

Effective Web design has three major stages: (1) requirements gathering, (2) experience design, and (3) usability testing. You start by figuring out what the website needs to do or include—what its "requirements" are. Next, you attempt to design a user experience that meets those requirements by creating a prototype. Then you put the prototype in front of real people and watch them try to use it.

The best sites tend to cycle through stages 2 and 3 in an iterative loop—with the sites' designers watching people use prototypes, redesigning the prototypes to try to improve the experience, and then observing as people use the revised site to see whether the changes helped:

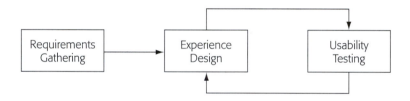

Requirements Gathering for a Portfolio Website

In the case of your portfolio website, requirements gathering involves deciding what the site should accomplish and whom it will serve. The term *requirements gathering* is just industry jargon for the process of figuring out what the purpose of a site is, identifying the site's intended users, and arriving at a list of what should be included. If you were identifying the requirements for a portfolio site, you would consider three factors:

1. The goals of the site's *owners*—which, in the case of your portfolio site, would be you.
2. The goals and needs of the site's *audience*, or users—in this case, the potential employers who may look at your portfolio.
3. The *human and technical resources* available for building the site. Unless you have friends who are experts in design and/or technology, don't identify any portfolio requirements involving features that you can't build yourself.

Portfolio Site Owner Goals

If you are creating a portfolio site, your goals as "site owner" are fairly straightforward. You want to convince potential employers that you have the skills and experience to work for them. More detailed goals might include demonstrating effective content on the Web, showing off a talent for visual design, or merely creating a convenient way for employers to see and download your resumé and examples of your work. Like a print resumé, an online portfolio is designed to communicate your abilities and experience. It should also demonstrate your communication and technical skills. Remember that your goal is not just to communicate your expertise but also to focus on what sets you apart from other applicants.

Portfolio Site User Goals

You have to know what kinds of people make up your audience before you can determine what they need. Depending on where you apply—whether avant-garde small business or conservative government agency—the people accessing your portfolio will have different priorities and expectations.

If your hiring managers would be likely to have a fine arts degree from a design school in New York City, they may have different expectations and judgment criteria than if they had an engineering degree from MIT. If possible, talk to a few people who are similar to your target audience and ask what matters to them about their selection process.

Human and Technical Resources

The requirements you set for your personal site will also need to take into account the human and technical resources available—namely, you. Don't get so ambitious that you end up with a project that would take even experienced experts in design and technology months to build. You'll also have to think about the technical constraints imposed by the organization that will be hosting the site. Some universities offer free space for student websites but limit the amount of storage to a few megabytes, which is just fine for a primarily text-based portfolio site but may preclude an extensive collection of high-resolution photographs.

Possible Content Items for an Online Portfolio

The requirements you set for your portfolio site will have a lot to do with who you are and what you know. We'd expect to see big differences between the portfolio for a graphic design student and one for an engineer. However, some possibilities for your portfolio items include:

- Writing samples—reports, business plans, proposals, news releases, brochures, usability reports, or other examples of your work. You may want to include them as PDF (Adobe's Portable Document Format) files.
- Databases or other programming or engineering projects you've created.
- Links to universities, previous employers, and courses.
- E-mail links to references—but *only* if you have permission to include the links.

- Graphics samples or artwork.
- Links to websites that you helped create.
- A downloadable version of your resumé in PDF.
- Awards.
- Course descriptions for courses that you have either taken or taught.
- Reference letters, if appropriate and if you have permission to include them.

Experience Design

If requirements gathering is about deciding what your portfolio site should include and why, experience design is about the details of how the site should be built. You'll find that you can't help but jump into the creative process when you have direct contact with users. If you succeed in interviewing a few hiring managers, the specifics you hear about how they make decisions will spark ideas for how to design your portfolio site to meet their requirements. These ideas can be a reaction to explicit needs ("I hate it when people don't let me download their resumé in Word") as well as some that are more implicit ("I don't want to see frills. Just prove to me that you've got solid experience"). If a majority of hiring managers in your desired profession require a Word version of your resumé, you'll obviously just include it. And if you hear an implicit conservative visual bias, you'll think about a straightforward design that allows direct access to your architectural drawings and leave the animated intros for another project.

Moving from a broad concept to a finished prototype is a progression from the general to the specific. Designing the user experience for your portfolio site will involve three design tools: (1) a site map, (2) wireframes, and (3) visual designs.

- **Site maps** are similar to the blueprints architects use to design buildings. Your portfolio site map will include:
  - The homepage
  - Major category pages, like "Recent Projects" or "References"

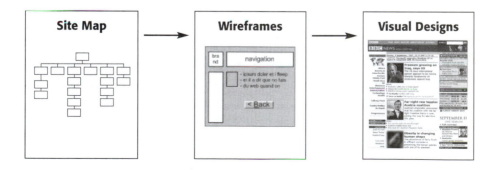

Site Map → Wireframes → Visual Designs

- Important subpages within each category, like "PDF resumé"
- Connections (links) between pages
- **Wireframes** are a more detailed blueprint of a single page. Used to plan information design, layout, and functionality, wireframes don't include visual design. Instead, they position features, functionality, and information objects (like blocks of text). You'll want to use wireframes to plan the layout of your portfolio homepage as well as the structure of major secondary pages.
- **Visual designs** express all of the visual elements in full color, as they will appear on the final pages.

Don't waste time early on tinkering with the design of individual pages. After all, some of the student portfolios we've seen have as many as forty pages. Instead, by evolving your experience design with the three design tools—site map, wireframes, and visual designs—you can focus your energy on major types of pages that have similar visual characteristics, such as the homepage, category pages, and content pages. That focus allows you to experiment quickly with different visual treatments on one or two page types. When you've settled on a design direction, you can then extend it to the rest of the pages in your portfolio without a lot of rework.

Creating a Portfolio Site Map

Your site map will help you decide how to structure the content and functionality in your requirements into an actual portfolio website. You have to figure out how many separate HTML (Hypertext Markup Language) pages you'll need, what to put on each page, and how those pages should relate to one another. Usually, we think visually about the problem. Using a whiteboard or pencil and paper, we draw a hierarchy of boxes with notations that represent individual HTML pages or PDF documents. We start with the homepage at the top and draw lines to represent links between pages. By keeping all the secondary category pages at the same level, and grouping any tertiary pages in clear subsets, it's easy to visualize your portfolio's structure, as in Figure 1.1.

This process of choosing how information and functionality will be organized, named, and navigated is called **information architecture** (IA). IA involves choosing labels and categorization schemes for your content.

The website categories in your portfolio may be topic-oriented (references, projects, resumé), task-oriented (download, contact me), or a mixture of both. In a strictly topic-oriented organization, headings, subheadings, page divisions, and links are based on the subject matter. In a task-oriented organization, headings, subheadings, page divisions, and links are driven by user tasks and goals.

Make sure your portfolio site categories make sense to users and play to your strengths. You want to communicate your experience as successfully as possible. If you taught English in Japan, don't label this "Teaching Experience" unless that's the most relevant label for the job you're seeking. If you're trying for a job

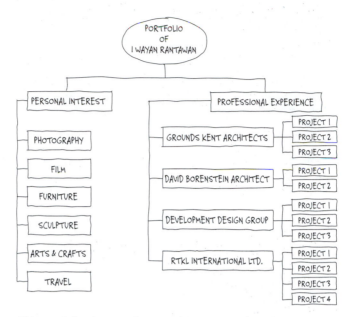

Figure 1.1   This portfolio site map by an architecture student shows how you can group secondary category pages and tertiary pages to enable you to visualize your portfolio's structure.

in industry, you may want potential employers to see this in terms of your "International Experience" instead.

Finally, keep in mind that a site map is not your site. Of course its structure makes sense when viewed as a map, because you can see the entire site in one glance. Users, on the other hand, will experience your portfolio only one page at a time. We speak in terms of "designing the user experience" to remind ourselves that although we're making decisions about navigation, labeling, and content, what matters is the user experience that results from all those decisions, not the structure or layout of the site itself.

Wireframes

Once you have created your site map and planned at a high level, you'll use wireframes to do more detailed planning about how to arrange items on individual pages. You don't need to make a wireframe for every single page in your site. But you will want to do wireframes of the homepage and each major type of page (such as category pages).

In your wireframe, you'll lay out areas for text, images, and any input fields—such as a form for entering name and address. Most sites also use navigation bars, with the global navigation across the top of the page and secondary (local)

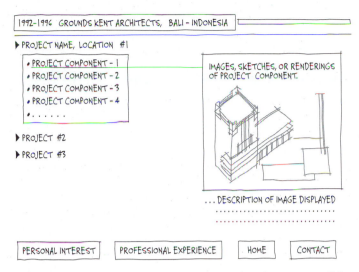

FIGURE 1.2   This hand-drawn example of a wireframe plans how items will be arranged on an individual page.

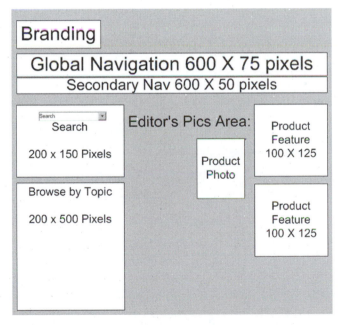

FIGURE 1.3   Computer-generated wireframes can define the size and placement of screen elements.

navigation either tucked underneath the global or going down the left side of the page in what webworkers call the "upside-down L." Navigation bars have become popular on the Web because linking words within paragraphs of text makes those links harder to find. When navigation bars are easy to read, are always located in the same place on the page, and have labels that make sense to users, they can make your site much easier to navigate.

Part of organizing your portfolio for success is making it easy for readers to act on what they see. A successful site structure supports and encourages user behaviors that are desired by the site owner (you). So if your goal for the portfolio is to get an interview or to get work, you need to make it easy for people to contact you by providing e-mail links wherever readers might feel the urge to use them. If you feel comfortable providing other contact information, make that information persistently accessible also.

Visual Design

Design matters. Take a look at Apple's iMac, the new Volkswagen Beetle, or even a Dr. Seuss book. Because of their design, these personal computers, automobiles, and books transcend the merely functional and border on the visceral: people *want* to use them because they have unique appeal. Design plays a crucial role in successful communication. It also establishes your credibility. Textured backgrounds, poorly utilized white space, or screen elements that blink will reduce the effectiveness of your portfolio and affect how potential employers perceive you. On the other hand, when the visual elements of your portfolio work so well together that everything seems to "fit"—guiding the eye through the site, clearly showing what's related, and reinforcing what's most important—employers will come away impressed. They'll not only remember the content; they'll also have a favorable impression of you.

Your site map and wireframes planned content in very general terms. But as you create your full visual design, you'll get specific. Dan Roam, an experienced interaction designer who works in New York City, suggests getting down to design specifics via three series of questions:

1. *Content:* What do you as the site owner want/need users to know? What do users want/need to know? Can you reconcile any conflicts or inconsistencies?
2. *Functionality:* What do you want/need users to be able to do? What do users want/need to do? When do they need to be able to do it?
3. *Branding:* What do you want users to remember about you or the site after they leave?

Your answer to this last question is particularly important, and we should stress that it matters whether you're an engineer, a triage nurse, or an architect. Branding isn't just for graphic designers. Think carefully about whether you want visitors to your portfolio site to remember you as innovative or meticulous, an idea generator or a more practical implementer. High-quality portfolio pieces can be undermined by a visual design that runs counter to their message.

Effective visual design means using visual elements to make the site content accessible, usable, and relevant to users. Your visual tools are color, layout, shapes, words, and images. As you create your portfolio's visual design, focus on the communication goals that will drive your use of these visual elements. Use them to

- Get the attention of readers and encourage them to keep reading
- Guide users through the site content by visually organizing the screen contents
- Focus attention on key information
- Show the context of information
- Help users find the site's functionality
- Increase the impact of the site or of specific content
- Set the tone and mood of the site
- Help define the site's audience

To create a visual design, you'll decide what words, icons, shapes, images, and so forth to include on the page. Then you will place these elements in relationship to one another. The spatial relationships among the visual elements of your portfolio have to support your effort to communicate. The most important elements should look important in comparison to the other things on the screen. Similar content items should look similar. The most frequently used features and content should be the most noticeable and the most readily available (things like your downloadable resumé, your contact information, and your work samples). The functionality of the site should be obvious, and navigational elements should look like navigational elements.

Keep your design consistent. Every screen of your portfolio site needs to be in harmony. Visual consistency increases user comfort and security, and it reduces the time necessary to locate and process information. Techniques for maximizing consistency and regularity include:

- Using a standardized color scheme
- Using a consistent layout that aligns or reflects visual elements along a common axis
- Standardizing or repeating sizes and spacing of elements
- Reducing elements to basic geometric forms, where appropriate

Finally, effective visual design does not necessarily mean elaborate design. Simplicity and minimalism are key components of good design—and they are particularly appropriate for a portfolio site. Unless you are a professional clown, nowhere in your site requirements would we expect the goal of "entertain" to trump "inform." The central criterion for every design decision should be whether it helps you communicate your message more effectively. Not only does every design element add to the cognitive effort required to use your pages, but it may also cause the pages to load more slowly. Make sure the gain in improved communication outweighs the cost for each design decision. The two portfolio sites in Figure 1.4 do a good job of achieving simplicity in design.

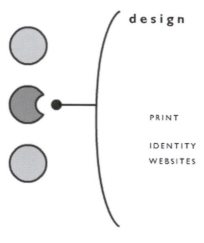

FIGURE 1.4   Both of these portfolio pages from visual designers find an effective, albeit different, balance between simplicity and design.

Effective Portfolio Content

Obviously, there was very little detail in your site map beyond page titles like "Resumé" or "International Experience." And although your wireframes were more specific in terms of layout, their written content was not very detailed—perhaps a box that said "intro text here." However, as you make the leap to final visual designs, you'll need to do some writing. Although much of the content in your portfolio site is already prepared—things like writing samples and your resumé—you will need to write introductory text, links, and other navigational text that is specific to the Web.

Writing for the Web is different than writing for print. The fact is, people don't really read text on the Web; they scan it (Morkes and Nielsen, 1997). It's not easy to read small fonts on a screen that's uncomfortably far away and has only so-so resolution. You'll want to design your text so that scanning it is likely to produce good comprehension and retention. Your goal is to help your readers get the information that they most need and that you as the portfolio site owner most want them to have.

The following guidelines (adapted from Jakob Nielsen and John Morkes) will make your text easier to scan:

- Keep text focused and concise.
- Use strong verbs and the active voice.
- Use lists.
- Use meaningful headings, subheadings, and summaries.
- Avoid hyped, marketing-style language with lots of adjectives.
- Use highlighted key words.

The degree to which you succeed in impressing potential employers will obviously depend heavily on the quality of the work examples you include in your portfolio. However, the *text* that may be the most crucial to the success of your portfolio is the short, introductory blurbs you write to introduce your portfolio pieces. These introductions help communicate the structure and organization of the portfolio itself and provide the rhetorical context for your portfolio pieces. Most readers won't read everything in your portfolio, but they are likely to read this introductory text. So you'll need to polish it until it is as clear and perfect as you can get it. Use the following guidelines to make your introductions effective:

- Orient your readers to what they're about to see; give them context for the piece.
- Talk about the purpose and audience for the piece and about the skills and tools you used to create it.
- Draw readers' attention to key elements of your piece, so that they are more likely to notice and appreciate your skills.

- If appropriate, emphasize your problem-solving abilities. Talk about each of your pieces in terms of the problem you were trying to solve. Briefly define the problem and suggest the symptoms or results of the problem (in about a sentence or less). Describe your piece as a solution to that problem and evaluate its effectiveness (without overt bragging, which would damage your credibility).

See Figure 1.5 for examples of effective introductory text.

Once the introductory blurbs are perfect, move on to your **nomenclature**—an industry word for the text used in headings, navigation, and links. Whether heading or link, your nomenclature is both a label for a chunk of content and an introduction to that content.

People should be able to predict what they'll get by reading that section or by following that link. Writing good link text is particularly critical: following a link takes time, energy, and bandwidth. If users are disappointed with the results of following one or two links on your portfolio site, they are less likely to stick around and try any more. Check titles, summaries, and headings after you've completed your prototype to make sure that they reflect the content as accurately and completely as possible. Place the link on the information-bearing word; avoid "click here." When accessing your portfolio, people will tend to scan from link to link, and you want them to be able to get a sense of your offerings just based on the link titles.

Once you've created a visual treatment that is effective, that includes excellent, scannable written content, carefully worded links, and consistent navigation, extend that design to all of the pages in your prototype and get it ready. Remember our three milestones for effective design? At this point, you've gathered requirements for your portfolio site and designed a user experience. Now it's time to observe someone trying to use your prototype.

Usability Testing

Even if you are an experienced interaction designer, your prototype only represents a first draft—your earliest attempt at responding to what you've learned about users with an interaction design. You now need to conduct a series of iterative usability tests—revising your prototype based on what you learn.

We'll go into a lot more detail about how to do usability testing in Chapter 6. But the key message is that you don't need a Ph.D. in human-computer interaction to do an effective usability test and improve your website. Although you may not perform all of the following steps in designing your portfolio site, we want to introduce the entire process at this point anyway:

The Usability-Testing Process

1. *Develop the test plan.* Create a list of tasks that you want a user to accomplish using your portfolio site while you watch. Possible tasks might include: "Find

Details

Stuart Moulthrop is Professor of **Information Arts and Technologies** at the University of Baltimore, where he directs the **Doctorate in Communications Design.**

His hypertext fiction *Victory Garden* (**Eastgate Systems**, 1991) has earned a place in Robert Coover's "golden age" of electronic writing. His **later projects** ("Hegirascope," 1995; "The Color of Television," 1996; "Reagan Library," 1999; and "Pax," 2003) belong happily enough to this age of brass.

Moulthrop has written many **essays**, including "**You Say You Want a Revolution?**", which brings up the rear in the *Norton Anthology of Theory and Criticism.*

He serves on the Board of Directors of the **Electronic Literature Organization** and is Emeritus Editor of the on-line journal *Postmodern Culture.*

He recently served as Program Co-Chair of the **2002 ACM Hypertext Conference**, held at the University of Maryland in June, 2002 and is currently a member of the Academic Advisory Committee for **Digital Arts and Culture 2003** (Melbourne) and the Foresight Panel of the **Information Technology University of Copenhagen.**

His *curriculum vitae* is available in **HTML** and **PDF**.

news · hypertexts · essays · teaching · talks · links · details · home

Hypertexts

Reagan Library   [1999] Published on CD-ROM as part of *Gravitational Intrigue*, the *Little Magazine's* electronic anthology. A circular exploration of time, space, and (imperfect) memory.

Hegirascope   [1995/1997] What if the word will not be still? Or worse, what's in the trunk? The first version of this time-based Web fiction was published in the now defunct *World3*. A revised version appeared in in *New River*.

Hypertext '96 Trip Report   [1996] This small non-fiction hypertext was an early experiment with JavaScript and multiple publication styles. It might also be considered a primitive ancestor of 'blogs.

The Color of Television   [1996] I created this multi-threaded, verbal/graphic Web fiction in collaboration with the writer and designer **Sean Cohen**. It was published in the "Lab" section of *Media Ecology.*

It's Not What You Think   [1995] A "multi-level hypertextual rant," says Steven Levy--and he should know. This little project may also have been the world's first hypertextual letter to the editor.

Watching the Detectives   [1994 and continuing] This non-fiction hypertext is an Internet companion to Alan Moore and Dave Gibbons' *Watchmen*. Developed for the Web in late 1994, revised with reader contributions several times since, and most recently converted by Nancy Kaplan to a database-driven form that allows readers to submit their own contributions.

Shadow of an Informand   [1993/94] I first wrote this early experiment in scholarly hypertext argument in non-electronic form, then ported it to HTML as one of my first efforts on the Web.

Dreamtime   [1992] This small hypermedia fiction is a refugee from *Victory Garden* and an earlier, abortive project aptly titled *Chaos*. It's a HyperCard stack, and as such is useful only to those who still have access to that software and a Macintosh that can run it.

Excerpts from *Victory*   [1991] This large-scale hypertext fiction was called by Robert Coover "the new

FIGURE 1.5   Portfolios don't have to be fancy in order to be effective. These pages come from the portfolio of a university professor.

and download my resumé"; "Review my portfolio of photographs"; or "Tell me about how informal or formal this site seems to you."

2. *Select and recruit participants.* In designing your portfolio site, you may not be able to recruit an actual potential employer to participate in a usability evaluation, but you want to find the most representative sample user possible. Try not to use roommates or friends, unless they happen to be representative of your target audience.

3. *Prepare the test materials and set up the testing environment.* If you have an interactive prototype, you'll want to make sure that all of the sections you want to test are built and ready to go beforehand. In regard to the testing environment, when you're in the professional world, you may have access to a sophisticated usability lab, but for now, all you need is a computer and two chairs.

4. *Conduct the test.* The way you moderate the test, assign tasks, probe for more information, and give off nonverbal signals to the test participants can have a huge effect on the validity of what you learn about your prototype. We'll go into more detail about these issues in Chapter 6, but for now, we'll just point out that it's very important to avoid leading questions and control your body language. Remember that you don't want to manipulate people into saying only good things about your portfolio site. Nor do you want to guide them to the "right answers." Your goal is to observe them behaving as realistically as possible on your site and note problems so you can fix them.

5. *Transform data into recommendations for revision.* You are going to find problems with your site—it's inevitable. Just note them and fix them. At the end of each session of your usability tests, you will debrief the participants and probe to have them tell you what went through their minds and what confused them. Listen carefully to what they say, but pay even closer attention to what they do. You'll be able to identify major usability problems and make adjustments to the site that try to solve them.

For your portfolio site, you will probably test your design no more than once or twice, with only a couple of participants. However, for most sites, we recommend doing multiple rounds of usability testing, redesigning each time so that the site gets better and better. For your next site, we'll ask you to do complete tests with six to eight users (see Chapter 6). When you are working for clients, you will quickly see the value of doing rapid prototypes of site ideas and using iterative usability testing to drive improvements with user feedback.

Ethics and Credibility

We've mentioned that a well-executed online portfolio will help you a great deal in developing credibility with potential employers. We also want to point out right in the beginning of this text that credibility is earned. As you've designed your portfolio, you've made hundreds of decisions about how to present information about yourself favorably. The pressure to "look good" certainly won't go away when you begin your professional life and start producing websites for your employer.

The most serious unethical behaviors in creating a Web portfolio include providing inaccurate or misleading information about your job experience or your qualifications or presenting other people's work as your own. In other Web design situations, you may be similarly tempted or even pressured to manipulate your data, use deliberately misleading or ambiguous language, exaggerate claims, or conceal information that your users need in order to make good decisions. However, succumbing to this pressure can have serious consequences, ranging from legal liability to loss of credibility and damaged relationships.

Unethical behavior in website design would also include plagiarism or stealing proprietary information. Even if you are given permission to borrow someone's code, you need to provide acknowledgment. You cannot legally use someone else's graphics or text without permission. (Chapter 5 discusses important ethical considerations in planning your Web content. See also the website accompanying this text for further discussion of copyright issues.)

To create a persuasive site, you must convince visitors that you know what you're talking about and that you mean them well. Without first establishing your credibility, you may have a difficult time persuading potential employers to act. The most powerful way to gain credibility is a genuine focus on user needs. Concentrate on what you can do for your potential employers, not on what the employers can do for you. As we've mentioned, professional-looking design and high-quality writing also enhance your credibility.

We invite you to hold yourself to the highest ethical standards as a site designer. We've learned through experience that in doing so, you will achieve far greater success than "bending the rules" could ever bring.

Looking Ahead

Now that you've had the experience of taking a portfolio site from concept to finished prototype, you're ready to look at effective website design methods in more detail. In the next five chapters, you will gather requirements for a client website, design the user experience, and engage in an iterative process of repeated testing and redesign.

As in the professional world, where no work begins without a project plan, you'll need to work out a rough schedule of the following tasks:

Requirements Gathering

- Identifying and analyzing the needs, business goals, and branding goals of the site owners
- Analyzing the site's users and their tasks and goals

Designing the User Experience

- Capturing your user research in task flows and concrete descriptions of your primary user types, called **personas** (explained in Chapter 3)

- Designing your site—creating a site architecture and paper prototypes
- Creating a working prototype

Testing for Usability

- Testing and revising your prototype
- Revising and editing the prototype to create a final version of the site
- Final testing
- Delivery (include the evaluation report from your final testing, if possible; it should show that you've done a good job)

As you schedule these activities, work backward from the due/delivery date. Whether your professor has you work on your own or in groups, you'll want to start making arrangements at the beginning of the semester for activities that will involve other people besides you and/or your team. Schedule your early user interviews, usability testing, and any necessary reviews of your content by outside experts. Plan for any resources you might need for the project, such as possible costs for scanning, color printing, or thank-you gifts for test users when you do your usability testing (discussed in Chapter 6).

> **Being an Effective Team Member**
>
> If you will be working on a website design project as a team, this would be an appropriate time to organize your team, plan for the resources you'll need, and schedule all the activities necessary to accomplish your goal.
>
> Your team will be more effective if each team member makes a formal commitment to do the following:
>
> - Come to meetings on time and be prepared.
> - Respond promptly to requests from team members. Make it clear that your work for the team is a high priority for you.
> - Communicate about problems clearly and professionally. Avoid excuses and complaining; talk directly to the appropriate person if there is a problem.

The next chapter, "Requirements Gathering," walks you through the process of deciding what kind of site you need to build and what it should include. What is it you want users to be able to accomplish using your site? How will you measure the site's success? Answering these questions effectively will become the foundation for designing an effective site that will meet the needs of both its owners and its users.

✔ FINAL CHECKLIST

User Focus

- Do you effectively communicate your experience and qualifications?
- Does your content focus on what your potential employers need or want?

Do you show users why your abilities and experience might be important to them, in terms of *their* goals and priorities?

- Are the contents of your portfolio arranged to meet the users' needs and priorities?
- Will your labels and categories help potential employers make sense of your experience? Do your headings and links allow users to accurately predict the content that they introduce?
- Do you maintain an appropriate and professional tone?

Introductory Blurbs for Portfolio Items

- Are your introductory blurbs brief and focused?
- Does the introduction to each portfolio piece orient users by providing context? Have you explained the purpose and audience for each piece?
- Have you drawn users' attention to key elements of your portfolio piece?
- Have you emphasized your problem-solving skills, as appropriate?

Information Architecture

- Is all the information that potential employers might need available right when and where it is needed?
- Have you provided multiple paths to important information, as necessary?
- If you have included multimedia, does it support your communication goals?
- Do your pages make sense out of context, in case users arrive somewhere in the middle of your site?
- If your pages require scrolling, have you made sure that the most essential information appears above the fold?
- Do you have permission to use any e-mail links, reference letters, or collaborative work that you have included?

Visual Design

- Do your content and layout support the relationship you want to build with users?
- Do your images contribute to the success of the site? Is their contribution great enough to justify the added download time? Are images labeled, as appropriate? Did you include good explanatory text using the ALT tag?
- Is your format consistent from page to page? Are headings and other key text formatted consistently?
- Have you used color appropriately to support your communication goals? Does it make your content easier both to access and to understand?

- Do your portfolio pieces display well? Have you provided warnings about download times, as appropriate?

Ethical Considerations

- Have you kept your content ethical, by avoiding exaggerated claims or misleading information?
- Have you included information about when the site was last updated, to help users evaluate the quality of the content you provide?
- If you borrowed graphics from another source, have you obtained proper permissions and provided proper acknowledgment?

Quality Control

- Have you eliminated spelling, punctuation, and syntax errors?
- Have your graphics reproduced well?
- Are all links current and functional?
- Do your pages display effectively in different browsers and on different platforms?
- Have you made it easy for users to contact you?

 **REFERENCE**

Morkes, John, and Jakob Nielsen. "Concise, Scannable, and Objective: How to Write for the Web." 1997. http://www.useit.com/papers/webwriting/writing.html

2 Requirements Gathering

CHAPTER HIGHLIGHTS

Site Owner Business Goals
  How Do Site Owners Make Money?
  What Is the Size of the Market Opportunity?
  Who Are the Site's Most Formidable Competitors?
  What Are the Specific Revenue and Growth Goals? How
  Will You Measure Success?
  What User Behaviors Best Support the Site Owners'
  Business Goals?

Site Owner Brand Positioning
  Who Are the Site Owners' Current Customers or Audi-
  ence? The Site Owners' Potential Customers?
  What Uniquely Ownable Benefit Does or Could the Site
  Owners' Brand Possess?
  What Tone and Image Do Site Owners Want Their Brand
  to Represent to Their Audience?

User Goals
  Observe Representative Users in Their Environment
  Debrief and Capture Findings—the Same Day
  Work in Cross-Functional Teams
  Confirm Your Hypotheses with Quantitative Research

Technical and Human Resources and Requirements
  Technical Requirements
  Human Requirements

The last chapter introduced the Web design process and gave you a chance to gain experience by creating a portfolio website. Now that you've done some hands-on work, you will use the rest of the book to learn the stages of Web design in more detail and apply them to a client project.

As we mentioned briefly in Chapter 1, requirements gathering is the process of determining what kind of website should be built and why. Ideally, a Web design project begins with consultation of stakeholders as well as research about end users and their needs—which are then captured in a **requirements document.**

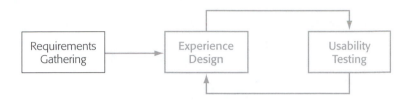

The document records what the customers or site owners need and what the design team has agreed to provide. In some situations, stakeholders review and actually "sign off" on the requirements document once they've agreed on its specifications. This process is intended to ensure that stakeholders have agreed—in writing—on the specifics involved in the new design.

Requirements gathering is one of the most important parts of the Web design process. It is also what separates excellent webworkers from average ones. The methods they use, and the time they take before a single line of code is written or a single design concept is considered, are what make the difference.

Whether you are an engineer publishing information about a robotics project, an architect who needs to create a site about a new project, or a full-time Web designer working for a client, you must follow a careful process to identify the requirements of what you should build. When you were creating a personal site for your friends about your vacation to Cozumel or your Gund® platypus collection, designing without requirements might have been tolerable. But in a professional setting, you have to take a more structured approach. Identifying requirements is about pursuing the answers to a series of important questions. The questions may differ slightly from setting to setting—university library, graduate class, or large corporation—but their fundamental nature won't change. The following sections present four categories of questions and considerations that you should discuss with your site owners:

1. Site owner business goals
2. Site owner brand positioning
3. User goals
4. Site owner human and technical resources and limitations

If you foresee yourself working in an academic or a government setting, you may look at terms like *business goals* and *branding* and think they don't apply to you. However, all sponsors of website projects, organizations as well as individuals, need a way of defining what constitutes success and how it can be measured. And if you think of branding as what you want people to remember about you, then even a marine biology site involves important brand-positioning decisions having to do with credibility and quality of research.

Site Owner Business Goals

A successful Web design team needs more than an eye-catching layout and usable navigation. Even if you're working for a nonprofit organization, understanding and setting business goals is a critical part of identifying the specific functional requirements that you or your site owners have for the new or redesigned website. Asking stakeholders a series of important questions lets you use their answers to help create the design. By getting these answers early, you can return to them later in the design process when things might otherwise have a tendency to get out of control.

But be careful. Relying too heavily on site owner ideas can get you into trouble. Stakeholders usually do a great job of articulating what they want the *outcomes* of their site redesign to be:

- "I want people to see my online portfolio and offer me a job with a big fat salary."
- "We want to have the best law library website in the country."
- "We want to be *the* pet supply retail destination on the Web."
- "We want to *reinvent* the concept of business financing."

However, site owners might struggle when translating those goals into specific details about what should be built and why. Rather than engaging in premature efforts to design the site itself, help your stakeholders focus on their business goals with the following series of questions.

How Do Site Owners Make Money?

Regardless of whether your stakeholders think of success in terms of money, you want to focus on what user behaviors actually support their organization's goals. If the goals are not specifically monetary, you might ask, "What must happen for us to be successful?" Library stakeholders might respond with, "Success means more library patrons paying overdue fines on our website than at the service desk." Not-for-profit stakeholders may say, "Success would be a 10 percent increase in the number of people who come to the site and decide to volunteer." Asking the money question is a great way to get decision makers focused, because they're usually familiar with that way of thinking.

What Is the Size of the Market Opportunity?

When trying to weigh the amount of time, technical resources, and money that should be spent on different parts of a site design, it is obviously helpful to know how much demand is out there. A 360-degree virtual-reality tour of a coral reef might be very interesting to the layperson, but if the vast majority of your marine biology website's audience consists of hardened researchers who are more likely to download findings quickly and leave, then the amount of time and equipment needed to create the coral reef tour deserves a hard look. Likewise, if research estimates that more than a million people are going to begin using electronic billpay in the next six months but only a few hundred thousand would ever be interested in expensive market-tracking personalization features, deciding which of the two to implement gets a lot easier.

Of course, a larger issue is whether there is market demand for the entire offering. Not every part of an organization belongs online, and not every online project will provide a good return on investment, no matter how well the site may be designed. Whether the organization sponsoring a particular site is a library, a church, or a retail store, there are some functions that succeed when enabled through the Web and others that don't. The primary driver, of course, is people. Are there enough people out there who want what you are offering? Find out as much as you can before including complex features in your requirements document.

Who Are the Site's Most Formidable Competitors?

Taking stock of the competition seems so obvious that it's almost not worth mentioning. But site owners should identify their major competitors before they determine requirements. Take a hard look at what competitors are doing and not doing with their websites. Then, as you identify requirements, evaluate how your offering will compare with theirs.

But watch out for the tendency to "keep up with the Joneses." During a redesign of a major airline site, the site owner's response to questions or discussion about requirements was too often "Delta's doing it." This reaction wasn't so much a competitive analysis as it was a knee-jerk impulse to declare that if other airlines did it, it must be a good idea. Of course, that's not always true.

What Are the Specific Revenue and Growth Goals? How Will You Measure Success?

You can't really convince yourself or your site stakeholders that the design or redesign of the site has been a success if you didn't begin the process with some goal in mind. Our best recommendation is to be realistic. During one site launch, a big-five consulting firm that was in on the project predicted that the site would have a million customers by the end of that year. It had 107,000. Don't just make up the numbers. Instead, try to connect them to some real metric of success for the venture.

If the site is owned by a nonprofit organization, do some investigating before the redesign and find out how successful users are at getting things done with the existing site. After the redesign, repeat the investigation. You hope to be able to show the site owners that, yes, users who visited the redesigned site were more readily able to understand its purpose (for example, fundraising or issues for education) and, yes, they were immediately able to make a donation.

If you're working with a corporation or a business, set success metrics relative to what the site owners are spending on site development. Of course, the site's results can far exceed expectations—and if you do things right, they probably will—but set some realistic metrics based on what the site owners are investing in the design or redesign. If your bosses are spending $800,000 on a redesign, break that down into numbers of new customers, reduced support costs, product sales, or some other measure. Estimate how many user behaviors the site owners need to see in order to recoup their investment. Managers appreciate this kind of thinking, and it will help keep you accountable, too.

What User Behaviors Best Support the Site Owners' Business Goals?

Instead of thinking about behaviors, some site owners want to start looking at designs right away. But wise site design teams will refuse to begin designing until they get a firm answer about user behaviors, because this issue is so closely connected to the site's success metrics. At first, some site owners may not know which user behaviors are most valuable to them. If there's uncertainty, go back to the first question—about how the site owners make money or measure success. Map backward from the outcome ("The library saves money on reference desk costs without sacrificing patron satisfaction"). User behaviors that would support the library's business goal might be for users to (1) notice that a reference service is available on the website and (2) submit reference questions successfully.

Site Owner Brand Positioning

While business goals and metrics focus on how an organization will make money—on identifying what specific product and service offerings will *satisfy* customers, prospects, and potential investors—brand positioning focuses on how to *approach* them. Sometimes when we teach mixed audiences about effective site design, those who work (or plan on working) in academic, government, or nonprofit sectors balk at the idea of branding. They mistakenly assume that their organization doesn't have a brand or that branding issues don't affect their website. That's probably because they're used to thinking of a brand as something that's exclusive to consumer products—like soap or DVD players. But branding is much more strategic than that. The Museum of Modern Art, the Internal Revenue Service, the Mayo Clinic, and Syracuse University all have brands. In the broader sense, a brand is a product, service, or concept that is publicly distinguished from other products, services, or concepts in the minds of consumers.

Branding means associating a product or service with core values that resonate with people. We can talk about a brand as consisting of the following:

- Brand promise
- Brand attributes
- Brand personality

The **brand promise** defines the primary benefit provided to customers that you hope will differentiate your product or service from the competition. The

brand attributes are the supporting benefits that customers receive from your product or service. These brand attributes may be functional (reliable, flexible, fast), emotional (trustworthy, friendly, fun), or self-expressive (helping customers feel smart, hip, or successful). The **brand personality** is how the brand expresses itself—how the brand is communicated to customers.

People are demonstrably more likely to buy or use products and services that are strongly branded, so a strong brand is a powerful, albeit intangible, organizational asset. Again, don't fall into the trap of assuming that brands are only for corporations. Do you think that organizations such as NASA, the Red Cross, Yale University, the New York Public Library, or even the United States government don't have brands that inform the way they approach people? Of course they do. Even job-seeking graduate students who create portfolio sites have brand attributes that need to be communicated effectively.

Sometimes organizations associate branding with the strictly creative elements—logo, identity, colors, and design—of their online approaches, but these elements communicate only the brand personality. To define the brand itself, you need to start with strategic issues—issues that matter for small organizations as well as large ones. Even if you are producing Web materials for the tiniest of two-year colleges, you want to pay attention to how you brand your offering. This process can be as simple as making sure the essence of your offering coincides with customer needs or as global as deciding which offerings or services fit into your brand strategy and which ones don't.

To help your site owners understand the branding requirements for their site and come up with a branding strategy, you need answers to the following questions.

Who Are the Site Owners' Current Customers or Audience? The Site Owners' Potential Customers?

If your project happens to be for a larger organization, its market research group may already have information about the segmentation and demographic distribution of its customers. If it doesn't, find out whether it can do some market research. As you position the brand and think about the design, you obviously need to understand whether you are talking to Generation Y, baby boomers, or both. If, on the other hand, you are working on a website for a small science library at a college in Maine and your site owners tell you that your market research budget is virtually nonexistent, you're not out of options. You can still talk to at least a few members of your "target market." Stop people in the foyer of the library and chat with them. Get the library to offer some promotion, maybe amnesty for late fees, for students who are willing to let you stop by their dorm rooms and watch them interact with the library website. Interview them about their perceptions of the library. Any information is better than none, even if it is just the qualitative insight you take away from several field observations. You can't begin to know how to approach your customers effectively until you know who they are and start to understand their needs.

What Uniquely Ownable Benefit Does or Could the Site Owners' Brand Possess?

Two pioneers in branding, Al Ries and Jack Trout (1981), said it best: "Positioning [branding] isn't something you do to a product. Positioning is what you do to the mind of the prospect." But before coming up with any kind of creative strategy, site owners need to define their brand. Large organizations will probably already have branding work you can apply to your Web project, but for smaller organizations, arriving at a brand definition means educating the site owners first.

A good example for helping site owners understand brand promise comes from the credit-card industry. Visa's uniquely "ownable" benefit (branding-speak for the distinctive benefit your brand seems to "own" in the marketplace) is ubiquity: Visa owns the idea, even if it isn't true, that it is the most universally accepted credit card. It's important to help your site owners understand that brand promise is different from the tag line ("Visa. It's everywhere you want to be."). Brand promise is the idea upon which the tag line is based. And it is broader, so that television commercials—and in our case, websites—can be designed in keeping with the brand.

This uniquely ownable benefit should then be the foundation for your site owners' brand promise. It explains *what people get* if they act. It is the single most compelling benefit (not product attribute) that

> **Wear Black . . .**
>
> Ask questions like these and your site owners and colleagues will think you used to work on Madison Avenue:
>
> - What are we branding?
> - To whom should we be talking?
> - What is their current relationship with the brand?
> - How did this relationship come about?
> - What is their relationship with the key competition?
> - What do we want people to think, feel, and do (rational/emotional/action)?
> - What will get them there (the bridge between the consumer and the brand)?
> - What is our uniquely ownable proposition (one thought or brand promise that we can own versus the competition)?
> - What is our support for this thought? What brand attributes do we need in order to fulfill our brand promise?
> - What is our brand's tone of voice (smart, hip, fun)?

will motivate people to act. It is usually emotional, not physical. People don't necessarily rely on feature-for-feature comparison when they choose to buy a Porsche over a Toyota. Nor is the decision based purely on dollars and cents. Berkeley and Harvard are both excellent schools, but people who are choosing between them don't make the decision solely on the basis of cost or even quality of education.

To help site owners develop their brand-positioning statement, have them begin with a list of attributes that focus on the functional, emotional, and self-expressive benefits they want people to associate with their product or service. When listing adjectives to describe these attributes, think carefully about each one and how well it supports the others. Then pare the list down to two or three words that convey the essence of the brand. Porsche = performance, prestige, power. Toyota = value, reliability, practicality. Using this pared-down approach makes it easier to understand the brand motivations that cause people to act. The brand promise and key brand attributes should shape every interaction with users.

What Tone and Image Do Site Owners Want Their Brand to Represent to Their Audience?

The brand's "personality" is how the brand expresses itself, how its promise and attributes are communicated to customers. The brand's personality may be the only factor that separates it from its competitors. When a purchase decision involves—or perhaps even depends on—an emotional response, a likable personality provides the necessary emotional link. A consistent brand personality not only helps the brand distinguish itself but also helps define the interactive experience that represents that brand online.

Smaller organizations that have never mounted a serious marketing campaign may not have spent much time thinking about their brand. The whole notion of "brand" may even be a new concept for them. In these cases, we use the question of tone and image to inspire site owners to identify two or three adjectives that they would like their customers to associate with their organization. Pinning your site owners down on even a few basic brand attributes will help you understand how to approach the requirements of the website.

For example, the *Wall Street Journal* doesn't use color photographs in its print edition. This has nothing to do with the relative communicative merits of color photographs versus black-and-white illustrations. It isn't a design decision. It has everything to do with how the *Wall Street Journal* wants customers and competitors to perceive it and, perhaps more important, how it wants its customers to perceive themselves—as intelligent, informed, conservative, and cognizant of the value of a newspaper that relies on text to communicate financial news and related information. USATODAY.com has a "Life" tab on its website; WSJ.com does not. That is a product/content decision that is driven as much by brand as it is by user goals. There are more than forty-five different colors on the USATODAY.com homepage. WSJ.com uses black or dark-blue text on a white background, with a few light-gray shaded tables (see Figure 2.1). These design decisions communicate how WSJ.com sees itself, but they also send a message about who the site designers think their readers are.

User Goals

A lot of site owners and their Web design teams pay lip service to discovering user goals. But for some, identifying user goals comes down to little more than the BOGSATT (*bunch of guys sitting around a table talking*) method.

You may not feel like it yet, but if you are designing a website, you are probably immersed in a relatively expert Web culture and cannot get inside the head of,

FIGURE 2.1　Visual design differences between WSJ.com and USATODAY.com reflect differing brand strategies. (See Figure 4.2 for a color version.)

say, a retiree who just installed AOL for the first time. So don't just try to visualize users or their experience. Although demographic descriptions or market segmentations can help a great deal, don't rely exclusively on them, either. Even focus groups are not enough. Focus groups remove users from their normal environment and context and put them in a room full of strangers, where they summarize their experience and behavior—leaving out lots of important detail. What users remember about what they do and what they actually do are sometimes different.

The best way to accommodate user goals is to design with specific people in mind. And we don't mean the fictional user profiles that some advertising agencies use. Instead, you need the rich detail that can only come from observing real people in their real environment—including the type of computer, available bandwidth, technical skills, jargon, and even workplace or consumer culture.

For the purpose of gathering requirements, there is a systematic way of discovering user goals that can be adapted to most situations.

PROFESSIONAL PROFILE *Janice (Ginny) Redish*

Studying Users in Context

President, Redish & Associates

You can't talk about user-centered design without talking about Ginny Redish. She is one of the pioneers. She began with a Ph.D. in linguistics from Harvard, and her initial usability research focused on the problems people have with workplace documents. In 1979, she founded and directed the Document Design Center at the American Institutes for Research, in Washington, D.C. In 1985, Ginny established one of the first independent usability test laboratories, and since 1992, she has worked as a consultant in usability and documentation.

Her two books are indispensable for anyone interested in user research or usability testing. *A Practical Guide for Usability Testing,* coauthored with Joseph Dumas, provides a practical introduction to usability testing, including how to plan and conduct tests, analyze data, and communicate and use results. *User and Task Analysis for Interface Design,* which she coauthored with JoAnn Hackos, takes readers step by step through practical ideas and techniques for observing and working with users before you design a product.

Ginny Redish and her colleagues have sent a powerful message to usability professionals, design teams, and business management: successfully designing a product to meet users' needs requires looking at actual users in their environment.

A couple of examples she shared with us clearly illustrate why. Early in Redish's career, she was working with a company that was designing a new application. It was to have a graphical user interface (GUI), to replace the command-line interface that the company's employees had been using, and was predicted to increase employee productivity dramatically. Management knew that the company would have to buy new computers in order to enable its employees to use the new application, but it still felt the investment would be worthwhile. From Redish's training, the design team's members realized that they had to go into the field to observe and talk with actual users. The team tried to get prospective users excited about the new application, but the users pointed out that although the new computers would be able to run the new GUI application, they would not be able to run other essential command-line applications. The users would end up needing *two* computers—one for the new GUI application and one for their older command-line applications. The users' small cubicles had no room for two computers. Members of the design team for the new application had thought only about their own product design; they had not thought about the other

continued on next page

work the users needed to do. After the field visits, the project was delayed and incorporated into the larger context of the users' workflow.

In another example, Redish and her team were working with a major airline in 1995 to design software that would support both travel agents and consumers. Among many other things, her team discovered that printing the physical ticket was a much bigger hassle for travel agents than had been realized. The machines that printed tickets were very loud, so they were kept in a backroom. The location of the machines meant that agents had to leave customers and go get the tickets. Tickets ordered by phone were printed at the end of the day in batches, which then required sorting and mailing, with the attendant possibilities for error. These observations helped motivate the adoption of something we all use regularly—electronic tickets. During that same project, Redish's team heard users asking not only for a way to search for the best fare on a particular day, which the software already enabled them to do, but also for a way to search for the day that would allow them to get the cheapest possible fare. Users wanted, for instance, to know "When in the next month would be the cheapest day to fly from Boston to New York City?" Current search engines, such as travelocity.com and expedia.com, now support this kind of searching.

Ginny Redish is unusually committed to nurturing other usability professionals and has received awards and honors from Association for Computing Machinery, Systems Documentation Special Interest Group, Society for Technical Communication, and Institute of Electrical and Electronics Engineers PCS. Look for her name at conferences and attend her sessions. You won't be disappointed.

Observe Representative Users in Their Environment

You don't have to have a Ph.D. in anthropology or be an expert in observational research to get out of your office, observe users, and ask them questions about what they need and want. The simplest way to find out what users' goals are is to (1) watch them and (2) ask them.

Get started by determining the kinds of people you need to observe and interview. Larger organizations may already have an understanding of the major user groups who are potential audiences for a website. For example, managers of a library may know that they want its website to serve students, faculty, and library staff—and if you were going to identify user goals, you'd want to interview and observe members of all three groups. If your site owners ran an e-commerce site that sold baby supplies, you might have user types like young parents, grandparents, and nonparent gift buyers.

After you've identified the user groups that you need to study—go after them. When Michael was at Scient, his team once worked on an urban culture site that was the brainchild of a famous basketball athlete, who wanted to create a site that reached urban minorities. At the time, Scient's office was in Union Square in New York City. So Michael walked out his front door with a video camera and began stopping people on the street and asking them questions about urban life and technology. The team's user research didn't end there, but it was an important first step in getting connected to real people and grounding early concepts in the reality of the goals of actual users, not just the goals of the site's owners.

To make your study of user goals most effective, you've got to remember your purpose. You ultimately want to identify the requirements of a website. You want to know what the user requirements are for the new design. Hugh Beyer and Karen Holtzblatt (1998) pose two big questions that can help you think about user research and the way it should inform design:

1. What matters to people about their process?
2. How should we respond?

Before you can skip to question 2—deciding what kind of interaction and website should be designed in response to user needs—you have to understand what matters to users about their process. By understanding what matters to students about their information-search process, for example, you can decide how to support that process online.

For a classroom project, you'll probably need to limit the number of user interviews and observations you conduct. For the average professional project, we like to talk to between seven and ten people from each user group. The key is to try to observe users where they actually live or work. In the library, for example, you might arrange to follow students searching for materials and then finish up with an interview about their goals.

Before we begin research, we usually create a list of questions or issues we want to understand (see the accompanying feature for some possible questions). We also plan a rough structure for our session. We prepare a packet in advance to explain the goal of the field visit, plan how we'll use the time, articulate the kinds of things we are looking for, lay down ground rules for preserving participant privacy, and take notes about user behaviors and comments. All those who attend a field visit—whether they are moderating, just observing, or actively taking notes—must read this packet and bring it with them.

For example, in a recent website project for a pharmaceutical company that sells over-the-counter medications, Michael visited young parents, experienced parents, and retirees in their homes. He divided each visit into three rough sections. The first section involved participants' giving his team a tour of their medicine cabinet, introducing the team to their children, and walking through their process for researching and choosing medications as well as for solving problems or answering questions (such as about dosage). Whenever possible, we like to begin our visits with observation rather than an interview. Because the team was in the participants' homes and every little Post-it note on the refriger-

Researching User Goals and Tasks

Questions for Researching Overall User Goals and Tasks

- What are the users' goals?
- What do users currently do (tasks) to achieve these goals?
- What are the user characteristics that might affect their work?
- What are the users' personal, social, and cultural traits?
- What previous knowledge do users have about the subject matter, tasks, or tools?
- What is the users' physical environment?
- How do users relate tasks to goals?
- What resources (help desk, information, artifacts) are available to users as they work?
- How do users interact with one another?

Questions for Researching Individual User Tasks

- What information do users need in order to do this task?
- Where do users get this information?
- What do users do when they get stuck?
- What are the steps of the task (task sequence)?
- What tools do users use now to perform the task?
- How did users learn to use these tools?
- How easy to use are the users' current tools?

ator was right there, users were able to be specific and sometimes show us their process in far greater detail than they would have been able to do in a focus group room. After the first half-hour of observation, Michael then sat down for a more traditional interview. We like to keep our interviews fairly unstructured—allowing the flow of the visit and the participants to determine much of the subject matter. We come prepared with five to ten questions that we know we need answered and allow the rest of the topics to emerge. In this case, Michael finished the visit by having participants take his team to their home computer to observe how they research over-the-counter medications online and attempt the very tasks they'd shown the team in the first half-hour—this time on the pharmaceutical company's website. As you can imagine, the design team learned a great deal about what mattered to people about their process.

It will be rare that you will build a website for an organization that doesn't already have some kind of Web presence. Instead, you'll probably be adding to an existing site or redesigning a site that the organization wants improved. In those cases, it makes sense to include some observation of users trying to accomplish their goals with the existing site so you can have them compare what they want to do with what is possible now.

P ROFESSIONAL P ROFILE *Shelley Evenson*

Conducting Research to Understand User Needs
Shelley Evenson

*Chief Experience
Strategist*

SeeSpace uses immersive research to uncover a rich set of data for designing the resources (everything from the color of a button to the sound of a picture being taken on a digital camera to a display of account options on an ATM) that people use in their interactions with technology. This research helps us understand users in natural settings without preconceptions—see their activities differently—and lets us build better experience resources and foster the best possible relationships between a business and its customers, employees, and partners.

We borrowed heavily from social scientists and others in developing our tool kit. Our research methods often employ "guerrilla" tactics, since we often have only a few days or weeks to gather information. When we choose a method for gathering insights, we ask the question "What will deliver the most information about the experience, the business, and the competitive landscape?" We also think about what will bring us closest to the ultimate end user. Whatever method we choose, the point is to provide an understanding of specific situations of use (for example, pushing a button) or position the experience in a broader cultural context (for example, a new way to clean clothes). Ultimately, the final mix depends on the unique goals and constraints of the project we are engaged in. The list below provides a glimpse into the kinds of research that we use to provide insight into user needs.

Observation

Observation can be captured or "live." The most common techniques for capture are video or still photography. Live observation is done in real time and usually recorded by notes or sketches in a field journal. We can be either a participant in the experience or an outsider. We usually participate in the activities by "shadowing" the user's daily routine (for example, following physicians as they do their rounds) or observing from a distance (for example, watching business travelers use their cell phones at an airport). Our goal is to immerse ourselves (and our clients) in the user's context. Direct observation provides data that lets us accurately see, document, and analyze activities, objects, and outcomes from the perspective of the user. It also helps us develop user profiles (or personas) that are drawn from actual user behavior and not just lists of demographic data relating to a particular segment.

continued on next page

> **User-Directed Data Gathering**
>
> For those times or situations when we can't be present, we direct people in gathering data about themselves. One way we do it is by giving users a disposable camera and asking them to photograph specific aspects of their life and activities. Another technique we use is journaling. This is where we ask users to keep a journal of their activities, objects they encounter, and the outcomes of their activities as they occur rather than by recollection. Sometimes journaling can be prompted by a pager, phone call, or specific time if timing is critical to understanding the nature of the experience. User-directed data results are similar to observation results but provide an individualized and intimate perspective on specific user activities.

Debrief and Capture Findings—the Same Day

On the way home in the car, or immediately after returning from a field visit, it's a good idea to "debrief" with everyone who attended and capture as much detail as possible while notes and memories of the experience are still fresh. Depending on the user population, we often use digital cameras or even digital video to capture behaviors and visuals. With one person acting as a scribe, type up a field visit summary (see Figure 2.2) that includes the following:

- Digital photo of participants
- Age
- Name
- Educational background
- Professional experience
- Description of a typical day in the participants' life
- People with whom participants collaborate and how they do so
- Domain knowledge
- Computer knowledge, Web experience, connection speed
- Four or five key findings from the interview regarding goals, needs, and what matters to participants about their process

In the next chapter—"Experience Design"—we'll go into detail about how to analyze what you've learned about users and translate it into specific website design ideas.

Work in Cross-Functional Teams

Throughout the design process, we strongly recommend that you work in cross-functional teams. In your future professional projects, try to have stakeholders

Elisa
President, NoNameCo

Interview Date: March 08, 200X
Facilitator: Michael Summers

Job Responsibilities:
• President – NoNameCo
Professional History:
• Worked at IBM when it moved to the indirect channel.
• Left to start a technical marketing company that was sold in 1998.
Educational History:
• MBA, Harvard University
Computer Literacy
• Moderately savvy with WinTel, some confusion between browser and operating system
Collaboration
• "Most of my interactions are with Dick, the Vice-President of Partner Sales. He's one of the Dealers. Spot is the Director of Distribution. Our National Account Manager is Jill."
Background
• NoNameCo is a shipper and distributor to NoNameCo. It has $80 million worth of nameremoved inventory in its warehouse in Memphis, Tennessee. It deals with 275 to 300 authorized dealers.
• Significant inventories are required because NoNameCo needs to fulfill orders to dealers, ARS program (refurbished suppliers), ASBC (NoNameCo Small Business Connection), and NameRemoved (via ChannelMax).

Key Findings
NoNameCo needs to establish business processes that support the indirect channel. It needs to get accurate information to the indirect channel in a timely manner and quicker turnaround time on product orders.
• "But I'd say that the difficulty is once you get outside the per-view of the people we work with, then it's difficult to get processes changed. It's hard to really get things developed fast enough to support the channel."
• "It's a domino effect. Informational flow from, let's say, a NoNameCo factory to their business-partner care center to us, to the dealer, to the end user...So that process needs to work more efficiently to get the information to our computers faster. More reliable data and more reliable information. That's critical to our dealers. But we have to cross several NoNameCo departmental lines. That makes it tough to get that information in a timely, accurate manner because you're going across several NoNameCo lines."
  "Then the dealers really need to have quick turnaround on all products. So for the price that we're able to keep in stock or to channel and assemble, we can turn around very quickly."

FIGURE 2.2   Capturing what you've learned in a field visit summary is a great way to distill observations while they're still fresh.

from business, technology, branding, and user experience go into the field to observe users together whenever possible. For a classroom project, you'll probably have to do your best to make users real and concrete to these stakeholders through your site visit summaries or even through edited video summaries.

Inevitably, business goals, technical constraints, brand strategy, and user needs come into conflict. For example, users of a university library website may say that they prefer to search rather than browse through the menus and choices the site has to offer. However, even if the library has the funds to buy the necessary software/hardware, it might not have enough human resources to implement the search functionality. Having a representative from the technical group involved in user observations will have two positive outcomes:

1. At least one "insider" on the technical team will see firsthand how badly users need the search capability, and that may have a positive influence on technology planning.

2. The design team will be alerted early on about technical limitations, which will help the team make informed compromises between what users need and what technology can deliver.

In another example, a team working on a national newspaper's website learned that users prefer direct access to all of the stories in each section (Sports, Politics, International News) directly from the homepage. However, the business goals of the site were to have as many opportunities to sell advertising as possible. Of course, advertising generated much of the revenue that made the entire operation possible. As a result, the Web team was obliged to require users to go to intermediate "section" pages (Sports, International News) before moving on to individual stories. The intermediate page made it possible to sell more advertising because users viewed banner ads on the homepage, the section page, and then finally the individual story page. In this example, business goals trumped user goals in a necessary compromise.

Confirm Your Hypotheses with Quantitative Research

Quantitative survey research is not always as expensive as you might think. Depending on the computer use patterns of your target audience, you might be able to get valid confirmation of some of the hypotheses that grew out of your qualitative field visits by conducting an online survey. There are numerous websites, such as harrisinteractive.com or zoomerang.com, that will host surveys for you. These services approach the process in different ways. Some require users to follow a link (from an e-mail) to the site. Others "push" the entire survey via e-mail to selected respondents and record the results when users submit their responses.

It's a good idea to get the advice of someone familiar with survey research so you can have confidence in your findings. Based on the size of your population, a randomly selected sample, and your response rate, you can design a relatively small study that provides valid results. Some site owners will be more accustomed to quantitative rather than qualitative studies. Despite the fact that survey research cannot provide as rich detail as field studies about what matters to users about their process, surveys can give you confidence that the hypotheses about wants and needs that you developed by observing seven to ten people generalize across your audience. If you've already been into the field and come up with hypotheses, quantitative validation makes it a bit easier to reach consensus about million-dollar requirements decisions. Better to find out early that you're headed in the wrong direction than to read about it in the papers later, the way online-only banks or some business-to-consumer clothing retailers have.

Technical and Human Resources and Requirements

Even after you figure out how your site owners are going to make money, perfect a brand strategy, and immerse yourself in the user context, you're not done with requirements gathering until you understand two major things:

(1) technical requirements and (2) whether site owners have the people to support the kind of site you want to propose.

Technical Requirements

You don't have to be a technical wizard to assess your technical requirements realistically. Start by auditing your site owners' existing technical resources. Make an appointment to meet with their technical team; you'll find that the team will not only know about the technical architecture but can also give you insight about user and business contexts you won't get elsewhere. Ask the technical team to walk you through the Web servers, application servers, Internet connectivity, and security infrastructure that underpin the current website. This knowledge will help you understand where you are and where you should go next. (For help, see the accompanying feature "Questions for Gathering Technical Requirements.")

Keep in mind that any new requirements you create will have to be implemented either by applying existing applications or tools or by buying or developing new ones. Be aware of any existing data systems that need to be integrated with the new website. In financial services or health-care sites, these technical requirements and limits can be extremely complex, and in the worst cases, the Web offering can be driven by the structure of the technologies that support it. We're not suggesting that the requirements-gathering process should stress technical over human needs. But being aware of the technical limitations helps you negotiate the political issues you may confront as you make recommendations. Doing your homework and gathering information about the technical environment can help you know what is possible and what you are actually asking site owners to change.

It's also just plain smart to be thinking early about technical implementation. Discuss the security strategy for the new site with

---

Questions for Gathering Technical Requirements

- What applications and tools need to be developed in order to deliver your services online?

- What are your current technology assets?

- Are there any existing legacy/back-end systems that need to be integrated with the website?

- What are the security requirements for the website (authentication, SSL [Secure Sockets Layer] encryption, digital certificates, and so forth)?

- What are the scalability requirements for the website (in terms of the number of concurrent users—one hundred, one thousand, or ten thousand)?

- Do you envision any specific Internet technologies—such as XML, Java, or streaming media—being used to improve your website and business?

- Who will be hosting the website?

- What are the core components (personalization, content management, orders, and logistics) you need as part of your e-business architecture?

- Is total cost of ownership a critical factor in your technology decisions?

the site owners' technical team. Do some rough estimates of the site's scalability requirements. Knowing whether to expect one hundred or ten thousand concurrent users will definitely affect your direction as you design the site.

Gathering requirements means anticipating all of the different touch points customers will have with your site owners' product. You may want to plan to separate content from presentation by using a technology called XML, thereby allowing you to deliver content to systems such as handheld organizers and mobile phones. In your interviews with the technical team, be sure to discuss the core components of the e-business architecture that you are considering. Items like personalization (the systems that make "My Yahoo" pages possible) and content management systems are expensive and will transform the technical layout of a site's back end.

Finally, when you are thinking about technology, think about money, too. For most of the organizations we've worked with, total cost of ownership is a huge factor in the ultimate technology investment. That means that as we go through the requirements-gathering process, we have to balance our technological, personnel, and other resource decisions with how much they will cost to implement.

Human Requirements

Do your site owners have the people to maintain what your proposal requires? You may want to consider that before you propose a site whose content or visual design would need to be updated every day or one that would require complex technical updates once a month. Total cost of ownership includes the people with the know-how to keep the thing running. And we're not just talking about technical folks. We're talking as well about the content experts, editors, and graphic designers who maintain the site and keep it fresh. Get a sense of what positions (and skills) are available, and discuss plans for future hiring. If your site owners realize that because of your careful planning, they can actually keep the site maintained smoothly after you're gone, they will be your best advertising.

✔ FINAL CHECKLIST

Site Owner Business Goals

- Have you focused your site owners on exactly how they make money? How they are successful?
- Have you identified and prioritized the business goals for the site?
- Have you accurately researched the probable size of your target audience? The size of your market opportunity?
- Have you identified your major competitors? Have you analyzed the strengths and weaknesses of their sites?

- Have you set specific goals for measuring success—for example, revenue or growth goals?
- Have you identified the user behaviors that will best support your business goals?

Site Owner Brand Positioning

- Have you defined your brand promise—the primary benefit that your brand offers to customers?
- Have you identified your brand attributes—three key adjectives that will define your brand (for example, hip, smart, fast)?
- Have you decided what the brand's personality should be? How it should express itself in tone and image?

User Goals

- Have you identified your current customers? Your potential customers?
- Have you interviewed or observed users from each of your major user groups?
- Have you observed users doing work in their normal environment?
- Have you analyzed the users' physical environment?
- What user characteristics might affect users' interaction with your site?
- What are your users' goals?
- What tasks do users perform to achieve their goals?
- What steps are involved in their tasks?
- What information do users need in order to perform their tasks?
- What matters to users about their current process?
- Do you need to confirm your findings with some quantitative research?

Technical and Human Resources and Requirements

- What technical resources do you have available?
- Have you identified any technical constraints that might affect your design decisions?
- How many concurrent users will you need to support?
- Who will host the website?
- Do your site owners have the people to maintain the site after you're gone?

REFERENCES

Beyer, Hugh, and Karen Holtzblatt. 1998. *Contextual Design: Defining Customer-Centered Systems*. San Francisco: Morgan Kaufmann.

Dumas, Joseph C., and Janice C. Redish. 1999. A Practical Guide to Usability Testing. Portland, Oregon: Intellect Books.

Hackos, JoAnn T., and Janice C. Redish. 1998. *User and Task Analysis for Interface Design*. New York: Wiley.

Ries, Al, and Jack Trout. 1981. *Positioning: The Battle for Your Mind*. New York: McGraw-Hill.

3 Experience Design

CHAPTER HIGHLIGHTS

Making Sense of Your User Data
    Personas
    Task Flows
Experience Design
    Creating the Information Architecture and the Site Map
    Wireframes
    Visual Designs

The previous chapter, "Requirements Gathering," looked at business, technical, branding, and user goals and how you decide what kind of website to build and why. Now it's time to get down to the specifics of building it:

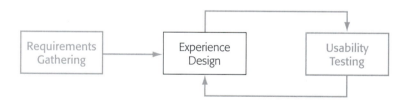

Making Sense of Your User Data

Effective experience design is a compromise among user goals, technical possibilities, business goals, and brand strategy. However, we make an effort to put users first whenever we can. During requirements gathering, you observed and interviewed the people who are going to use your website. Your next step is to analyze what you learned and translate user insights into design ideas.

User personas and *task flows* are tools for analyzing your user research. Both help you analyze what you've learned about users and make it easier to decide what that learning means in terms of actual website design directions. When we're getting down to deciding the details of a project, we want to be able to refer to users by name and ask some tough questions: "Would a 'Carmelo' really do this?" "Elisa says her most important goal is figuring out how much money she *really* has. Shouldn't her balance reflect the fact that her Mini Cooper car payment comes out automatically tomorrow morning?" Using personas and task flows can help you keep your design process user-centered. Without them, it can be tempting to forget what you learned about real users and make snap decisions based on what is easiest technically or what those with political power—that is, the people writing the checks—want to do.

Personas

By observing and interviewing users in their context, you developed a rich understanding of the people who are going to use your site. Part of effective design involves acknowledging an important fact: human beings are complicated. There are personal, social, and cultural factors that affect people's willingness to use websites. Just because you put a wireless laptop in the cab of each truck in your company's fleet doesn't mean that drivers are actually going to use your new intranet "properly" to keep track of customer visits or anything else.

If your professional life involves regular website design work, you will probably observe some arguing. Many organizations we've worked with have had a tough time resolving conflicts about what to do with their websites. When various power structures within the organization try to argue for one design direction over another, you will regularly hear an appeal to what users want. We've heard, "Users want X!" tossed across conference tables, only to be countered with, "No, they don't. Users want Y!"

Alan Cooper (1999) is known in website design circles for a tool he developed to try to reduce confusion about what users want and resolve conflict about design options. Remember that, in Chapter 2, we encouraged you to discover user goals by observing representative users in their environment and then capture what you learned in field visit summaries. Cooper's method synthesizes what is learned about individual users into user archetypes, which he has dubbed *personas*.

What Are Personas?

A persona is an archetype representing the behavioral goals of a particular group of users, based on field interviews and observation. Designing for a persona focuses the design to meet the needs of that persona and all the users he or she represents. For example, when car manufacturers design cars, they design for specific types of drivers. Otherwise, automobiles would try to meet too many needs and would satisfy no one. When he describes personas, Cooper (1999) asks people to imagine a sports car convertible with the cargo space of a minivan, the speed and sleekness of a roadster, the power of a V8 engine, and the efficient gas mileage of a motorcycle. Would anybody want to purchase such a

Professional Profile *Alan Cooper*

Using Personas to Guide Design

Founder and Chairman of the Board

Bill Gates dropped out of college. But Alan Cooper, one of the world's leading interface designers, actually dropped out of high school. A self-described "child of the sixties," Alan says it took him four years to figure out that just because people had told him he was going to be a "hippie loser" for the rest of his life, that wasn't necessarily his future.

Instead, he registered at the local community college, went on to found his own software company, and was responsible for an array of remarkable inventions, including a visual-programming platform called Ruby, which he sold to Bill Gates. (It's now the "visual" part of Visual Basic.)

For the last decade, Cooper's consulting firm, Cooper, has helped high-tech product companies integrate interaction design into their business and design practices. He uses an amalgam of ethnographic research, workflow analysis, and requirements gathering based on his years of experience in software and product design. His two books, *About Face: The Essentials of User Interface Design* and *The Inmates Are Running the Asylum,* are well known in the fields of Web and software design as sources of useful insights about why high-tech products often fail to meet customer expectations and how to solve this problem.

One of Cooper's better-known contributions to the field of interface design, the concept of *personas,* had its beginnings at a Chili's restaurant over a cheeseburger lunch with one of his early consulting clients. Alan discovered that although his clients could describe their technical design to him in great detail, they could say very little about their actual users. Over and over again, he would ask, "What do your users do with your product?" And repeatedly, his clients' answers would go something like, "Well, our new product's features mean they can use it to do X, or they can use it to do Y." Although they could think of things people *could* do based on the product's features, his clients didn't know any specifics about what users actually *did.* So Alan got names of current and potential customers and visited them. He didn't have a set agenda, but after he observed and interviewed about five or six users, several quite-pronounced patterns emerged. No one user was fully representative of an entire pattern, but each was partly representative, so Alan combined what he saw from individual user characteristics into three hypothetical users and gave them fake names: "Cynthia," "Rob," and "Chuck." He returned and helped his client prioritize its design for those "user personas," and the results were dramatic.

continued on next page

Alan's advice for students who want to design for the Web is to divide their experience between human-computer interaction classroom work and active collaboration with real software-engineering students. He emphasizes the importance of learning how busy engineers are and how little they care about "ease of use" unless solid reasons are provided for design decisions. He adds that businesspeople are interested in the bottom line—and won't be moved by impassioned speeches about user-centered design.

Alan is an adviser to the UC Berkeley Institute of Design and is active in several professional groups, including the American Institute of Graphic Arts, Association for Computing Machinery's special interest group on computer/human interaction, the Experience Design Forum, the Industrial Design Society of America, the Society for Technical Communication, and the Corporate Design Foundation.

vehicle? By trying to meet the needs of all drivers, such a vehicle satisfies none of them. A car that is inflected toward a particular driver will have multiple features (cargo space, good handling, power, and so forth) but will be *prioritized* for the target driver.

In Web design, personas help guide decisions about site features, navigation, interaction, and even visual design. By designing for the archetype—whose goals and behavior patterns are well understood—you can satisfy the broader group of people it represents. You will synthesize your personas from your field interviews and observations of current and potential users of a website. Persona descriptions include behavior patterns, goals, skills, attitudes, environment, and a few fictional personal details—pulled from your user interviews when possible—to bring them to life (see Figure 3.1). For any single website, one persona will be the primary focus for the design. However, a proper set of personas will remain complex enough to exhibit a wide variety of human behaviors and concerns.

Your **primary persona** should represent a large user group that is important to the business success of the site and whose needs may require special attention, such as Steven in Figure 3.1. A **secondary persona** might be John, an emergency room nurse who takes care of less urgent patients. For some websites, you may also need a **complementary persona,** with radically different needs, such as Peter, the billing coordinator, who uses patient treatment records to make sure patient insurance claims are properly filed.

For example, Michael worked on a consumer health-care site recently that had to support young mothers as well as retirees. Their needs and goals were as different as their familiarity with vocabulary and their ability to use the computer. After field visits in user homes, the team analyzed their data and created task flows and personas. As the design team made decisions, they regularly asked questions like, "When Cassie [the young-mother persona] faces this situation, what does she need to know first?" or, "Given their computer skills, will Jean and John [the retired-couple persona] realize that more symptoms and

Cooper's Tips to Remember When Creating Personas

- *Personas represent behavior patterns, not job descriptions.* A good persona description is not a list of tasks or duties; it's a narrative that describes the flow of someone's day as well as the individual's skills, attitudes, environment, and goals. A persona answers critical questions that a job description or task list doesn't, such as: Which pieces of information are required at what points in the day? Do users focus on one thing at a time, carrying it through to completion, or are there a lot of interruptions? Why are they using this product in the first plce?

- *Keep your persona set small.* You should use the minimum number of personas required to illustrate key goals and behavior patterns. Each persona should represent a set of usage patterns that are very distinct from those of your other personas. Although there's no magic number, even when the website you're designing is for a broad consumer audience, if you have as many as a dozen personas, then you may be making distinctions that aren't very important.

- *Understand your personas' goals.* Each persona should have three to five important goals that help focus the design. Goals and tasks are different: tasks are not ends in themselves but are merely steps we follow to accomplish goals. Three types of goals have relevance to design:

  1. **Life goals** are high-level goals that are only occasionally useful in design. For example, "retire by age forty-five" would be of little use if you were designing a word processor, mobile phone, or personal digital assistant (PDA), but it might offer valuable insight when you're designing a financial-planning tool.

  2. **Experience goals** describe how the persona wants to feel when using a product. Having fun and not feeling stupid are typical experience goals. Other experience goals might center on the product domain. A persona using an online banking site, for example, might want to feel confident that transactions made on the site are secure.

  3. **End goals** are the most important. These goals focus on what the persona expects to achieve using the product or service. End goals may involve the work product that results from using the tool. For example, graphic designers using a layout tool might want to create an award-winning ad. End goals can also involve indirect benefits from using a product. If managers want to be more proactive, a better spreadsheet tool can help them achieve this goal if it increases their efficiency.

conditions are available under the expandable secondary navigation?" There was a natural progression from the task flows and personas to design insights and problem solving.

Task Flows

A **task flow** is a graphical breakdown of the inputs, objects, actions, decisions, and results of a process. During experience design, the goal of creating task flows is to trace important processes and capture them in a visual. You can create high-level task flows about an entire organizational process, such as how a small company looks for business financing (Figure 3.2), or at a more detailed level, such as how a physician searches for a patient's prior EKG (Figure 3.3). (See the website accompanying this text for basic flowchart symbols.)

Steve Merrick, 36

Emergency Room Physician
Baltimore, Maryland

"Sometimes every second counts."

Steve Merrick is an emergency room physician at the Johns Hopkins Bayview campus. He got his M.D. at Johns Hopkins twelve years ago and has been working in the emergency room for nine years. He works three twelve-hour shifts a week, on a rotating schedule. When he's on duty, he often has to diagnose problems and prescribe treatment very quickly. If he has a question about symptoms or treatment, he typically needs answers in three minutes or less.

Steve married Kari about two years ago. She teaches physical therapy at Towson University. They recently purchased a large, gracious, three-story nineteenth-century row home with spiral staircases, wide-plank wooden floors, and molded-plaster ceilings in Bolton Hill, a charming Baltimore neighborhood. Steve owns a Mazda Protégé convertible, but he mostly takes the Baltimore metro to work. Kari drives an Acura Integra to Towson four days a week. Both Kari and Steve have agreed that they'd like to start thinking about having a baby. But Kari isn't sure whether to take a leave of absence from her teaching job.

Steve's work schedule is grueling. After a twelve-hour shift, he sometimes sleeps a full day. He knows that he needs to stay on top of new developments in medical research and technology, but coping with constant emergencies doesn't leave him with much energy for poking around on the Bayview Library site. It's easier for him to get news about important research from his colleagues.

Steve's goals:

- Make accurate diagnoses.
- Make effective treatment decisions.
- Maintain the energy he needs to do his job well.
- Start a family.

FIGURE 3.1   Personas are archetypes that represent the behavioral goals of a particular group of users. Because they have definite backgrounds, names, and personalities, they help keep everyone focused, stop repeated speculation about what users want, and guide decisions about site features, navigation, interaction, and visual design. When you design for a persona, your design is more likely to satisfy the broader group of people represented by that archetype. The details you'll use to build a persona should be specific (Steve needs to make a diagnosis in less than three minutes) and relevant to your website.

Building your personas through a brainstorming session that involves the full design team and key stakeholders can be a good way to generate excitement and build commitment to your project.

You create task flows as a team, by combining the results of all your individual observations. After your field visits are completed, assemble your summaries and call a meeting of all the team members who participated. If you have access to a classroom with a whiteboard, use that; if not, pick up some large newsprint pads from an art store and get ready to doodle. Start diagramming the results of everyone's observations. Your first goal is to document the current process as accurately as possible. You'll use your detailed understanding of the current task flows as a springboard to new design ideas as well as a reality check that your proposed designs will really work.

Accurate and specific task flows help us think about the potential structure of a new website in informed ways. We try to understand the details of the tasks as well as what users need in order to accomplish each step. If the task is to transfer funds

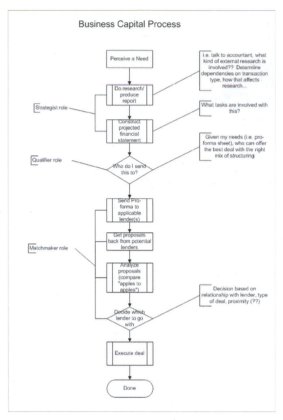

FIGURE 3.2   This task flow captures the high-level process that companies follow when they're seeking new business financing.

between accounts, there is specific information users must have in order to move from stage to stage. First, they need to know what accounts exist (checking, savings, money market), then the amount of funds in each account, and so forth. Failing to provide the information in the right order can obviously cause problems.

Even if the task is as simple as locating and printing directions to the university library, it is still useful to map out each decision point in the process. A relationship between the directions and library hours might be discovered before any coding or design work is even begun, allowing the system to be designed with both pieces of information on the same page.

In another example, Larry Marine, a well-known interaction designer and founder of Intuitive Design, tells the story of how user observation and task flows helped his firm improve a flower-delivery site. In creating task flows, his team noticed that the step of writing a gift card came after the unpleasant

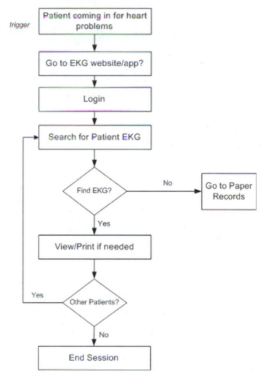

Locate Prior EKGs of Patient

FIGURE **3.3**   Detailed task flows can capture each specific step or decision point in a process—as with this example, which depicts the process of locating a patient's EKG from a medical library site.

step of entering credit-card information and that, worse, users were asked to provide credit-card information before they saw their total. During observations of customers ordering flowers in real stores, he observed the satisfaction and warmth people felt in writing gift cards. Making the gift card the first step in the task flow and requiring the credit-card information later in the process immediately reduced the number of abandoned shopping carts and increased the company's sales.

Task flows help you identify what key information objects—date of birth, overdue-book fees, account balance—people use and what criteria they employ to make decisions at various points in their process. A detailed understanding of their process helps you design effectively.

PROFESSIONAL PROFILE *Larry Marine*

Why Task Flows? A Success Story from the Real World
Larry Marine

Intuitive Design

One dark and stormy night, a purveyor of floral gifts rapped on my door. It seems that the company had too many people bailing out of its website in the middle of the purchase sequence.

The client's business model depended on a certain percentage of visitors starting the purchase process—let's say 20 percent—with 99 percent of them completing the purchase process successfully. Unfortunately, the company's original design approach resulted in about 2 percent starting the process and 30 percent completing it. Mind you, these were the industry norms at the time, but management knew that the company couldn't succeed on those numbers.

Our user research and the resulting task flows and user profiles identified key users as males buying a single gift (with an added accessory now and again) for females on a specific occasion. The first thing we did was introduce bundled gift items specific to each occasion, such as a Valentine's Day special and a birthday special. This simplified the men's process of figuring out what arrangement would be appropriate for women on a given occasion.

Our investigation also identified the main reason for purchasers' bailing out of the purchase sequence. We noticed that users were asked for their credit-card information immediately after deciding to purchase the gift. This violates average consumers' expectations about conducting a financial transaction, in which they expect to complete all of their shopping tasks and be given a total amount prior to handing over a credit card. In this case, the credit card was required prior to having a total. In essence, we realized that the credit card *must* be the last thing users do.

Although the reason for the early credit-card request given by the technical team made sense, it violated the users' expectations. The system needed to create a unique identifier for the transaction record, and the common method was to use the transaction-authorization number as the identifier. However, this number is only created after the credit card has been authorized.

Here is a case of the user experience and the subsequent business objectives being severely affected by a minor technological constraint. The solution was quite simple. We knew we had to move the credit-card request to the end of the sequence yet still create a unique identifier. Our suggestion was to create a temporary record until the credit-card authorization number was obtained.

continued on next page

Having moved the credit-card request to the end of the sequence, where users expect it, we then had to decide what step should go right after the users' decision to purchase the gift. Flowers are almost always accompanied by a gift card. Our user observations in a brick-and-mortar environment established that users fill out the gift card while the clerk is ringing up the sale. We made the online task flow match the offline behavior and allowed users to choose and write a card as the first step in the checkout process.

This one change dramatically improved the conversion rate. Usability testing showed that once the men had written something on a card, they were emotionally tied to the gift and they actually wanted to complete the sale quickly, waiting in anticipation for the credit-card screens, which they saw as the completion of the purchase.

In summary, when we made it easy to select the right gift, moved the credit-card screens to the end of the sequence, where users expected them, and used the gift card to emotionally support the purchase decision, users were much more likely to complete the purchase. Sales results after the changes showed that significantly more than 50 percent of the visitors selected a gift item and more than 90 percent completed the purchase.

The site is now one of the top e-commerce success stories on the Web. Its profits are in the tens of millions of dollars and growing.

Experience Design

Now that your task flows and personas have given you a sophisticated understanding of what matters to users about their process, it's time to decide how to respond—to identify what aspects of their process should even be addressed by your site and figure out what kind of interaction should be created. Three design tools will guide the transition from the general to the specific: (1) a site map, (2) wireframes, and (3) visual designs.

- *Site maps* are similar to the blueprints that architects use to design buildings. Site maps vary in detail, but they usually represent:

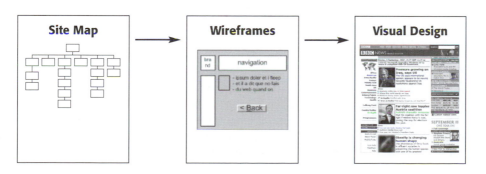

- Major pages and processes of a website
- Inputs and outputs that are possible on each page
- Connections between pages

- *Wireframes* are a more detailed blueprint of a single page or page type. Used to plan basic layout and functionality, wireframes don't include graphic design. Instead, they position features, functionality, and information objects (like blocks of text). Most early wireframes don't even include content, only boxes or areas that are mapped out to reserve space for content that will be developed at a later time.

- *Visual designs* (sometimes called design comps) arrange all of the visual elements in full color, as they will appear on the final site. Visual design is covered in the next chapter.

Be aware that the lines separating these three tools are fuzzy. Some site maps are large enough (we've seen wall-sized) that they include wireframes of major pages. There is also some variety in the industry regarding how detailed wireframes should be in specifying layout and positioning items on the page. For the purposes of this text, we'll describe the most common examples of each tool that are used in the industry.

Creating the Information Architecture and the Site Map

Choosing how information/functionality will be grouped, organized, and navigated starts with what is called information architecture (IA) and ends with your decisions' being documented in a site map. Information architecture involves determining the labels, categorization scheme, or navigation of your site. It also means designing processes that fit user skill levels, needs, and context. Information architecture is half library science and half software interaction design.

We first describe how to use card sorting to involve users in structuring the site's information and functionality and then talk about how library science has helped information architects think about information organization.

Card Sorting

Armed with your task flows and personas, as well as an understanding of the business and technical requirements you developed in Chapter 2, you're ready to begin drafting the structure of your site. One tool we use to figure out how to arrange things is card sorting.

Card sorting helps you understand how representative users group information objects and functionality. You can do card sorting in several ways. One way is to take all of the major information objects and decision points from your task flows and put them on cards. Then have users sort them into groups that make sense to them. After they've decided what items are similar, you can have users name the groups they've made. As you do this with several people, you'll get a sense of how they associate objects and processes as well as what category names make sense to them. This is called an **open card sort**. After the card sort, look for the dominant organizing principle underlying the groups and labels created by users. This organizational scheme can suggest an information architecture for your site.

Another way to do card sorting is to design your information categories first, based on your task flows and user profiles. Then give representative users information objects and functionality cards and have them sort using your predefined groups, as shown in Figure 3.4. This second approach is a **closed card sort.** Either approach is an effective way to catch problems early on, even with a fairly small number of representative users. For example, while doing work for a major sports league, Michael's team did a card sort in which one of the categories was "Store." The intention was to sell autographed sports equipment, team apparel, and so forth. However, most respondents placed search results or favorite statistics in that category, assuming that it was a place to "store" things. So the team modified the category name to "Shop," and users were able to sort correctly.

Organizing Information

If it doesn't make sense to pull your information categories directly from your task flows or user profiles, you can apply some useful approaches to organizing information that come out of library science. Richard Wurman, David Sume, and Loring Leifer (2000) have coined an acronym to help us remember common categorization schemes—*LATCH:*

> *Location:* Organize coffee brands by place of origin or the businesses in an office building by floor.

Figure 3.4 **Card Sorting** This picture shows a user sorting cards with information objects or functionality items under the headings where she would expect to find them.

Alphabet: Organize items alphabetically by name. Structuring information alphabetically can be an easy way to organize and access large bodies of information, as in a telephone directory, but it is not helpful unless users already know the names of the items they seek.

Time: Organize events in a process by sequence, such as a history of the Brooklyn Bridge or the steps in manufacturing a car. Organizing events by time can make it easy to discuss changes or make comparisons.

Category: Organize books by genre (romance, mystery, fantasy, science fiction) or retail goods by purpose (laundry supplies, personal hygiene, children's clothing). Categories work best if they don't overlap and if they are used to sort items of roughly equal importance.

Hierarchy: Organize academic programs at a university in terms of size of enrollment (largest to smallest), or organize cars from the least expensive to the most expensive or from the smallest to the largest. Hierarchy is based on comparison, and it arranges items along a continuum of importance, size, expense, and so on.

Your organizational scheme will then be represented in a site structure. See the accompanying feature for an introduction to some basic site structures.

Lou Rosenfeld and Peter Morville (1998) point out that the first three of these organizational methods—location, alphabet, and time—are unambiguous and fairly easy to create and maintain. The last two are the tough ones, because they require us to think, analyze, and make decisions. Yet, with conscientious effort, all of these methods can be used to organize information in ways that support your personas' goals and activities. Alphabetical schemes are best for known-item searches, whereas categories and hierarchies are particularly helpful for users who don't already know exactly what they want.

Rosenfeld and Morville discuss three useful ways to conceptualize categories:

1. *Topical:* Headings, subheadings, page divisions, and links are written based on the content topics they contain. An example of topical organization would be the yellow pages of the phone book or the range of products and services provided by a company.

2. *Task-oriented:* Headings, subheadings, and links are written based on user tasks. For example, the labels and menus of a software application are typically organized under task names. Designers must identify a group of tasks that will be important to users, and find task names that will make sense to users, before their task-oriented organization will work. An example of task orientation might be an online banking site, with tabs for checking your balance, making a payment, transferring funds, or adding a payee.

3. *Audience-specific:* Some websites that serve distinctly different audiences may sort their content into categories based on the particular needs of each audience. Thus, a university's website may have sections designed specifically for prospective students, current students, alumni, current employees, and prospective employees. Similarly, a mobile-phone company's website may have

---

Site Structures

Here's a short introduction to basic information structures that will help you get started.

Hierarchy   Hierarchies are organized on the basis of categories. Each category provides an overview or a preview of its subcategories. In a pure hierarchy, all items at the same level are the same type. In a lattice hierarchy, a topic may have more than one parent topic. You can also have a hierarchy with cross-references.

Linear Sequences   Sequences are easy to create and easy to comprehend; they are predictable, reliable, and simple. They can also be restrictive and frustrating, of course. (Horton [1990] points out that most of our experience is sequential: moments follow moments, words follow words, steps follow steps, paragraphs follow paragraphs.)

A good sequence has to make sense to the target audience. You should make sure that all the elements of the sequence are logically related and placed in a logical order (for example, you might use LATCH). Sequences (with possible side excursions) can be good structures when users will be trying to learn something.

Web   In a pure web, every topic is linked to every other topic. This is conceptually easy for the designer but not usually very helpful to users. They face too many links, too many choices. Navigation becomes confusing. However, it might be useful to employ special cases of the Web structure (for example, a partial Web or a star).

---

sections for business customers and home customers, which may be further subdivided into prospective customers and current customers.

Building the Site Map

Your next step is to use a site map (see Figure 3.5) to outline the structure of the site, including the section and subsection names, and to plan how users will navigate. Site maps also help us keep track of what functionality needs to be created and how various systems talk to one another to create a user experience that makes sense. Because they're the first step toward organizing the structure, site maps are useful if you're building a new site from the ground up or, as is more likely these days, if you're adding functionality to or redesigning parts of an existing site. A good place to start a site map is on a whiteboard, where you can erase easily. After you've developed a pretty good draft, you can then move to Word, PowerPoint, or a flowcharting application like Visio. Some information architects have collaborated on a standard visual vocabulary for drawing site maps (see the accompanying feature, "Site Structures").

Begin your map of the information architecture with the homepage. There are always a lot of things competing for space on the homepage, but we try to support as many top user tasks as possible right there, so users don't even have to navigate. We then determine the major site categories (and corresponding global navigation) based on what we learned from card sorting and insights from field research.

The decisions you make about information architecture will have a lot to do with the purpose of your site. Some sites pack literally hundreds of items on their homepage, because the purposes of site visitors may be so varied that

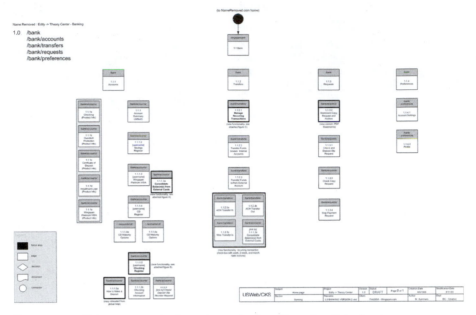

FIGURE 3.5   Site maps are used to create a basic outline of a site's structure.

hiding things behind global navigational choices creates headaches for users. For example, the Yahoo! homepage had 248 links as of our last count (see Figure 3.6). If you're looking for something that is buried in the middle of a large group of links, you can begin to feel as if you're playing a game of "Where's Waldo?" However, given the broad goals of Yahoo! as a search engine and Web portal, some users may find it preferable to have to hunt for a while. At least they have confidence that "Weather" is somewhere on the homepage. Some might prefer hunting to hitting the "back" button when they've guessed wrong.

Some usability research (Rosenfeld and Morville, 2002; Norman, 1988) indicates that users prefer broad, shallow sites rather than narrow, deep sites:

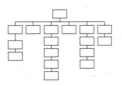

Other research indicates that users prefer not to be overwhelmed with hundreds of links. In practice, the breadth versus depth of your information and the number of links you use is a judgment call that will be affected by all of the forces described in Chapter 1: business strategy, user goals, technical limitations, and brand strategy. Google has a radically different approach than Yahoo! Instead of a portal offering, Google focuses on one user task: search. As a result, its homepage has 237 fewer links (see Figure 3.7). Whether Google's information architecture is "better" or not depends on your goals.

Occasionally, site redesigns involve fairly stringent technical limitations that can drive information architecture. Regardless of what we learn about how users think, we may have to make compromises because of those limitations. For example, Michael once worked on a banking site that actually had different back-end vendors handling the fulfillment and

> **Jesse James Garrett's Visual Vocabulary for Information Architects**
>
> Information architects have a recurring need to communicate an overview of site structure to other team members. One member of the IA community, Jesse James Garrett, has advocated a more standard visual vocabulary for IA work, and in collaboration with many other information architects, he has created a simple vocabulary that can be used either for hand sketches or with a variety of software tools. This vocabulary can be used to communicate site structure—including paths, actions, and the results of user interaction with the site.
>
> These symbols can represent the following:
>
> - Pages and files
> - Connections and paths
> - Concurrent events
> - Continuation points
> - Decision points, conditional elements, and multiple-choice branches
> - Areas or grouped pages
> - Special-condition areas or grouped pages
> - Reusable components such as flows
>
> His symbols are available from http://www.jjg.net/ia/visvocab/ as downloads for the following software packages: Visio, PowerPoint, Adobe InDesign, Freehand, Illustrator, IGrafx, and Flowcharter.

transactions for each of the different "tabs" in the global navigation. Although he and his team found that it made much more sense to group certain functions together, they were limited in how they could change the information architecture of the site.

Information architecture can get complex. However, there are many sites that do it well. BBC News and Britannica take very large sets of information and provide multiple ways for users to browse and find related items. Banana Republic presents items in categories that make sense and does a good job of allowing users to browse through its collection while providing a smooth shopping task flow.

One important information architecture development is the use of the relational database. You may have found a book at Amazon and seen at the bottom of the page "Customers who bought this book also bought . . ." The technology that makes that recommendation possible is called a relational database. One

FIGURE 3.6   The yahoo.com homepage is an example of a very broad and shallow information architecture. The result is more than 240 links on the homepage.

FIGURE 3.7   Google.com is an example of a search-dominated information architecture. There are obviously far fewer links on this homepage than on yahoo.com.

site that applies the relational database quite effectively is allmusic.com. Type in a favorite artist and you'll get the types of history and background you can find in any number of places. However, it is the "Related Artists" section that impresses, showing you relationships between the artist you know and ones you may not have heard of who have similar styles.

Planning Navigation

One serious danger of the site map as a design tool is that it gives the design team a view of the site that is not realistic. Of course the site makes sense when you can see all its components simultaneously! But we can never forget that (1) users are encountering this interaction for the first time and (2) they can only see one page at a time.

Our goal is to create an online navigational space that makes it possible for users to understand:

1. Where am I?
2. How did I get here (and how do I get back)?
3. Where can I go?

Let's use amazon.com as an example of how (1) a site map helps plan the structure, (2) wireframes are used to plan individual pages, and (3) visual designs complete the experience design process. An extremely simplified site map of amazon.com may look something like Figure 3.8. The navigation is hierarchical. Many sites have similar information architecture, with "global" navigation options available throughout the site and "local" navigation choices available only inside particular sections. In this case, the global navigation choices are "Books," "DVDs," "Music," "Toys," and "Photo." The local navigation choices ("Best-sellers," "New Releases," "Bargain Books," and "Rare & Used") appear only when we're in the "Books" section.

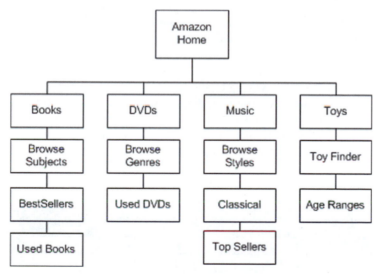

FIGURE 3.8   Simplified amazon.com Site Map

Most sites put the global navigation across the top of the page and either tuck secondary (local) navigation underneath the global or place it along the left side of the page in what webworkers call the "upside-down L."

Navigation bars play a central role in making your site easy to navigate. Effective navigation bars are easy to read, are always located in the same place on the page, and have labels that are meaningful to users.

When we know that something is important enough that users need access to it from anywhere, we may include it both on the homepage and in the global navigation. For example, you may highlight something in a "feature area" on the homepage and still include it as a choice in the global navigation.

Navigation can be noun-based and reflect the different sections of a site, or it may be task-based. In the navigation bar from an online banking site (Figure 3.9), verb-based navigation ("Transfer Funds," "Bill Pay") has been mixed with noun-based ("Accounts," "Customer Service"). We don't necessarily have a problem with that. Because the task flow within each of these sections will probably involve several user inputs and system outputs, it makes sense to have global access to functions like accounts or customer service. The most often used navigational tool on the Web is the "back" button, but to rely on it here would require users to click back through numerous unhelpful screens on which they had only entered amounts or pressed "OK." Sometimes, in highly transactional sites, the pages that users just visited "expire" because the data that populated those pages is temporary. In such cases, navigation bars become very important.

Wireframes

Once you have created your site map and planned at a high level, you'll typically use wireframes to do more detailed planning about how to arrange items on individual pages. Plan the location and size of text areas, images, navigation bars, and input fields—such as fields for entering name and address.

We should point out that site maps vary in the amount of detail they contain and that some site maps do include a certain amount of basic page-level planning. Depending on what you're trying to do, your site map may contain very few specifics beyond a page title, or it may get into a lot of detail about page content. You don't need to make a wireframe for every single page in your site. But you will want to do wireframes of the homepage and each major type of page (such as category pages and product pages).

FIGURE 3.9   Navigation Bar from an Online Banking Site. Note that some of the navigation tabs are noun-based and some are verb-based.

If we created a homepage wireframe based on our simplified amazon.com site's information architecture, it would look something like Figure 3.10. Remember, a wireframe isn't a complete visual design. Instead, it is a planning tool that helps us decide what we have room to include on a page and how the specific user interface controls might work. Your wireframes should reflect the work you've done designing task flows and identifying what functionality and information objects will appear on each screen.

Wireframes can be prepared in a program like Visio or PowerPoint, or they can be hand-drawn paper mockups that help you plan your layout and refine your strategic focus. A wireframe, like the ones shown in Figures 3.10 and 3.11, is a tangible representation of your planned layout.

Whether you choose to hand-draw your wireframes or create them digitally, understand that the point of a wireframe is that it's easy to generate and revise. It allows you to see whether or not your design is likely to work and lets you move things from page to page easily.

In the early stages of your visual design, you probably won't include content text in the wireframe; instead, you'll use mumble text, or what designers call "greeked" text, to give the visual impression of text.

In order to design your layout, you must have a clear sense of what content you have to include and how it is organized, but before you can proceed with the actual design and evaluation process, you need to step back from the specific information you're presenting in order to evaluate the conceptual relationships that are implied by the visual structure of the page.

To start your wireframes, make a list of all the items you need to display on each screen. Identify elements that will have to be repeated from screen to

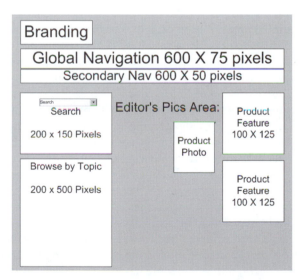

FIGURE 3.10   A wireframe helps you plan what information and functionality you'll include on each page—as in this simplified example of amazon.com's homepage.

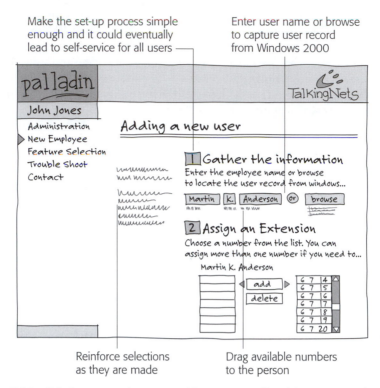

Make the set-up process simple
enough and it could eventually
lead to self-service for all users —

Enter user name or browse
to capture user record
from Windows 2000

Reinforce selections
as they are made

Drag available numbers
to the person

Figure 3.11   Wireframes can be prepared in a program like Visio or PowerPoint, or they can be hand-drawn paper mockups. Either approach helps you plan your layout.

screen. Group similar items. Assign priorities based on your business, branding, and user goals: What should users notice first? What should be available but not prominent? Make sure you pay particular attention to the placement and design of action items, such as input fields or cross-reference links.

If you find yourself trying to fit too much onto each screen, go back and reconsider your site architecture. Remember in Chapter 2 when we talked about business, user, and technical goals' coming into conflict? Well, it's during the wireframe stage, when details start being hammered out, that those competing interests really begin to make themselves felt. Your job is to ensure that the screen design does a good job of balancing those competing interests in order to make the site successful.

The last thing we'll say about wireframes is that there is a fuzzy line between where IA ends and visual design begins. Part of the purpose of a wireframe is to communicate the planned structure to clients, programmers, and visual designers. As you embark on your career and move from organization to organization, you'll find that in some places, different people have control over basic layout and the prioritization of objects on the page. Depending on where you work, you may have the freedom and responsibility to take your idea all the way through these stages from site map to wireframes to visual designs to finished prototype. However, some organizations divide up the labor and can afford to hire more specialized webworkers. If your organization has the budget to hire a visual designer with a masters in fine arts, that person isn't going to want an information architect to present a detailed layout to which the visual designer merely applies color. Negotiating a work method that allows mutual input into information design decisions and IA can be a delicate art, and you'll need to feel your way around each organization to find out how those decisions are made. For the purposes of this text, we'll proceed on the assumption that you will be doing everything, but know that when you get out into the field, that may not necessarily be the case.

Visual Designs

The final step in designing the user experience is to create a visual design for each of the pages in your site map. This process is the focus of the next chapter. Once you have a visual design prototype, you'll need to test your information architecture with actual users, as discussed in the chapter on usability testing. You'll make improvements and then test again.

Figure 3.12 shows what our Amazon example actually looks like, including visual design. You can see that the sections labeled "Product Feature" in the wireframe (Figure 3.10) now have content in them—an electric toothbrush and features for what's new at amazon.com and new music releases. The homepage

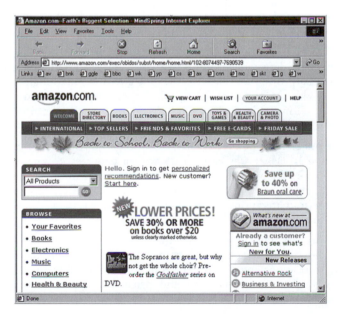

FIGURE 3.12 This visual design of amazon.com represents the final result from the site map (Figure 3.8) and wireframe (Figure 3.10).

<P<sub /> rofessional P_{rofile} *Hoa Loranger*

Using Paper Prototyping
Hoa Loranger

User Experience Specialist, Nielsen-Norman Group

One of my most successful projects involved paper prototypes. Our team was tasked with integrating a new feature into an existing Web application. We didn't have a lot of time and wanted to know right away if we were on the right track. We decided that paper prototyping would help us identify big usability issues (such as navigation and workflow) early in the design process.

Our paper prototypes were simple hand sketches created with common office supplies such as colored markers and sticky notes. Since each team member specialized in a different area, it was natural for the team to have divergent ideas on what the interaction model should be. Rather than commit to a single design, we sketched out our ideas and then tested them on actual users.

We asked the participants to interact with the paper prototypes. For example, they clicked by pointing to the area (a button, for example) on the paper prototype and typed in fields by writing in the information. One member of the team played the role of the "computer" by simulating how the interface would behave. I facilitated the sessions while the rest of the team observed and took notes. The prototypes engaged users, and they really got into it!

We made modifications to our prototypes after each round of testing. In this particular project, we started out testing two different designs. Then we combined what we learned to create a single prototype and tested and modified it several more times. We found glaring usability issues after the first round of testing. We kept the parts that worked and tossed out the bad parts.

Often our changes involved sketching up a few new screens or modifying content and labels. It was easy to do with a paper prototype. Our goal wasn't to make the prototype attractive and complete but to make it interactive. Coding started only after we felt that we had resolved any showstoppers. After four iterations of paper prototyping, we then tested the real interface to catch any additional surprises.

Paper prototyping helped us save many months of wasted development time by allowing us to test our ideas in the early stages and make changes quickly. Most important, it facilitated collaboration and buy-in among team members by giving everyone a fun and visual way to participate and contribute ideas.

doesn't have "local" secondary navigation, so Amazon has decided to repeat some of the options in the global navigation bar in a table on the lower left to increase the likelihood that users will find sections like "Books," "Music," and so forth.

As you design sites, you may choose to apply your tools differently. For example, you may make more detailed site maps that include some page layout. You may choose to evolve your wireframes through several iterations, perhaps including actual content such as text and labeling before moving on to visual design. However, most usability testing should be done on actual visual design versions of the site pages even if they are rough prototypes.

When you've been involved in the design process from the beginning, going into the field to observe users, interviewing stakeholders to get business requirements, creating user personas and task flows, and working out the site map, you have amassed a huge amount of context that may make wireframes seem clear to you. However, stakeholders who are seeing design concepts for the first time may not benefit from all that context, and we've observed radically different responses from real users who interact with the "same" page in wireframe as opposed to full visual design form.

In the next chapter, we'll go into more detail about how to take the wireframes you've developed and apply effective principles of visual design.

 FINAL CHECKLIST

User Personas

- Does your persona description include user goals, attitudes, and priorities?
- Do you describe the cultural and social factors that affect user decisions?
- Are users' work environment and workflow adequately described?
- Are your personas solidly grounded in your user observations and field visits?
- Have you chosen a primary persona as the focus for your site design? Is your persona set small enough to keep the design focused yet large enough to adequately reflect the complexity of your target audience?
- Does each persona have three or four important goals that help focus the design? Have you used the right goals? Do your persona goals describe what the persona expects to achieve using the site (end goals)? Do you identify how the persona wants to feel while using the site (experience goals)?

Task Flows

- Do you have task flows for all relevant user tasks?
- Do you represent all inputs, outputs, actions, decisions, and results of each relevant task?

- Have you identified all the information users will need in order to complete their tasks? Does your site design provide this information in the right place, at the right time in the process?
- Do you support users' expectations and priorities about how tasks should be structured?

Information Architecture

- Is the site content arranged to meet users' needs and priorities?
- Do both content categories and your content labels make sense to users? Have you employed the users' vocabulary as much as possible? Have you tested your content categories and labels with actual users?
- Is all the necessary information for each task available right when and where it is needed?

Site Map

- Have you represented all the major pages and processes of the site?
- Have you provided multiple paths to important information, as necessary?
- Are the possible inputs and outputs of each page represented?
- Is any planned multimedia content appropriately represented?

Navigation

- Can users tell where they are in the site? Have you tested this with actual users?
- Can users tell how they got to a particular point and how to get back?
- Can users easily identify places to go within the site?
- Are global navigation options consistent throughout the site?
- Are local navigation options clearly understandable as being local?
- Are navigation options labeled in ways that make sense to users? Have you tested them?
- Are navigation bars easy to read and consistently placed?

Wireframes

- Is your format consistent from page to page?
- Have you made sure that all your planned page elements fit on the page?

REFERENCES

Beyer, Hugh, and Karen Holtzblatt. 1998. *Contextual Design: Defining Customer-Centered Systems.* San Francisco: Morgan Kaufmann.

Cooper, Alan, and Robert M. Reimann. 2003. *About Face 2.0: The Essentials of Interaction Design.* New York: Wiley.

Cooper, Alan. 1999. *The Inmates Are Running the Asylum: Why High Tech Products Drive Us Crazy.* Indianapolis: Sams.

Horton, William. 1990. *Designing and Writing Online Documentation: Help Files to Hypertext.* New York: Wiley.

Norman, Donald. 1988. *Psychology of Everyday Things.* Cambridge, Mass.: Basic Books.

Rosenfeld, Lou, and Peter Morville. 2002. *Information Architecture for the World Wide Web.* 2d ed. Sebastopol, Calif.: O'Reilly.

Wurman, Richard Saul, David Sume, and Loring Leifer. 2000. *Information Anxiety 2.* Indianapolis: Que.

4 Elements of Effective Visual Design

CHAPTER HIGHLIGHTS

Defining an Overall Look and Feel
    Consistency
    Simplicity
Creating Page Designs
    Showing Relationships, Guiding Users Through the Site
    Visual Grouping—Gestalt Principles
    Designing Content Elements
    Layout
    Evaluating the Success of Your Design
    Designing the Homepage
Capturing Design Decisions in a Style Guide
Getting Ready to Test

In the last chapter, you and your team worked to distill the site's content into categories that made sense and to plan roughly what would go on each page. Now you have to communicate that information in a consistent look. Effective visual design means using colors, layout, graphics, navigational elements, interactivity, and interface metaphors to make the site's content accessible, usable, and relevant to users. Visual design is how you communicate your information architecture to users, how you make the site's content available.

Visual design plays a large role in establishing your credibility as a design team. Users may not stick around a site with bad visual design long enough to discover its hidden uses. Poor visual design annoys and frustrates users and can mark you as an amateur. However, slick design won't do you a bit of good with users if your site doesn't support their needs and goals. If the information architecture isn't well designed, or if the content isn't valuable, then even outstanding visual design won't save your site.

Jack Davis and Susan Merritt (1998) define three hurdles of user engagement that you need to address through your visual design:

1. *First second:* Communicate that your site is useful and well crafted.
2. *Next ten seconds:* Convince users that your site is easy to use.
3. *Next minute:* Convince users that you have interesting content that they can access easily.

Look at Figure 4.1. Does this homepage persuade you that the Dell site is useful, well crafted, and easy to use and that it has valuable content that is readily accessible? Does it feel inviting?

Defining an Overall Look and Feel

You start creating your visual design by choosing a general direction and goal, based on the audience information and branding goals you defined in the requirements-gathering phase. What overall look and feel does the site need to have? Remember the different visual branding goals of the *USA Today* site and the *Wall Street Journal* site we discussed in Chapter 2 (see Figure 4.2). Are you trying to be elegant and impressive, or hip and exciting? By the end of this chapter, you should have complete visual designs—first on paper and then as electronic prototype pages—for each major kind of page in your site.

Your primary visual tools are words, icons, shapes, images, colors, and layout. All of these will be shaped by the visual look and feel you choose for your site. As you start drafting paper prototypes for your site, you need to focus first on the communication goals that you hope to achieve through your use of these visual elements. As we noted in Chapter 1, you will employ these elements to

FIGURE 4.1   Dell's home site must quickly convince users that it is well crafted, easy to use, and has valuable content.

FIGURE 4.2   Design differences between USATODAY.com and WSJ.com reflect differing brand strategies.

- Get users' attention and encourage them to keep reading
- Guide users through the site
- Guide users through the information on each individual screen (visually organize the screen contents and successfully communicate that organization)
- Focus users' attention on key information
- Show the context of information
- Help users find the site's functionality
- Increase the impact of the site or of specific content
- Set the tone and mood of the site
- Help define the site's audience

Consistency

To maintain your desired look and feel throughout the site, every screen on the site must be visually consistent. Avoid what Web designers call "stylistic whiplash." Visual consistency increases user comfort and security, and it reduces the time required to locate and process information. The site's navigational elements need to be particularly intuitive, predictable, and easy to find. Visual elements such as boxes and arrows and the size, style, and treatment of text elements such as headings, captions, or call-outs should all be consistent.

Techniques for maximizing consistency and regularity include using a standardized color scheme, using a consistent layout that aligns or reflects visual elements along a common axis, standardizing or repeating the size and spacing of elements, and reducing elements to basic geometric forms, where appropriate. Keeping your site consistent will be simplified by incorporating your style decisions into a **style sheet,** which allows you to define the color, size, and format of selected webpage elements for an entire site. By including a link to the style sheet on every page in the site, you can make sure that each page in the site will be formatted in the same way by the user's Web browser. See the website accompanying this text for an introduction to creating style sheets.

Typically, you'll want to use different layouts for different kinds of pages. For example, you may have category-overview pages, detail pages, action or data-entry pages, or even "see also" pages. But even though the layout may change for different types of pages, you'll need to maintain an underlying consistency in order for your site to feel unified. Create a paper template for each kind of page, then an electronic template that can be used for adding content (the next chapter will talk about how to make your content as effective as possible).

Simplicity

When it comes to visual design, *effective* and *elaborate* are by no means synonymous. Simplicity is typically a key component of elegant design. Every design element you use should contribute directly to your success in communicating with users, because every design element adds to the cognitive effort required to use your pages.

Keeping the design simple will also help you minimize the time it takes to load your pages. Design elements that would help you communicate more effectively in a world of broadband access can frustrate (or even drive away) users if they make the pages load too slowly for users without broadband.

According to Kevin Mullet and Darrell Sano (1995), visual design is about communicating information in a way that is both effective and aesthetically pleasing. By combining principles of good information design with principles of good visual design, you can achieve this goal.

Creating Page Designs

In planning the visual design of your screens, your primary focus should be to make sure that the main objects of interest to users at any given point are visible on the screen. One of the cardinal principles of good information design is that information must be available when and where it's needed.

Second, the organization and presentation of that information should reflect users' needs and goals. The features and content areas that are used the most should be the most noticeable and the most readily available. That means you'll use size and placement of your visual design elements to show relationships and communicate hierarchy. When the elements on the screen are viewed as a whole, elements that are the most important should *look* important, and items whose content is similar should *look* similar. The visual design of the page should invite readers to move through the page's content in a useful and logical way.

Third, the screen design should make the site's functionality available to users. Navigational elements must look like navigational elements; interactive elements must invite interaction. Action areas need to appear near where users are likely to be looking when an action or a decision is required. The visual design should help guide users through the task at hand.

In this section, we talk about how to use your visual design to help users prioritize what they see, identify important elements, recognize logical groupings of information, and flow naturally through the site's content. Your goal is to use shape, size, color, and placement of text and graphical elements to help users answer the following questions:

- "Where is the object that I need?"
- "What is this item that I'm looking at?"
- "How do I perform this task?"
- "Where am I?"
- "What's the big picture?"
- "What other information is available that might help me?"

You use the visual characteristics of your content elements to make visual connections, to communicate a visual hierarchy. Perception is an active rather than a passive process. In other words, we don't just look at a page or a computer screen; we actively organize what we see. We resolve ambiguities, impose structure, and make connections. In a poor design, the visual cues on the screen can sometimes lead viewers to structure the information in a way that is different from what the designer intended. If the visual structure is incomplete or haphazard, users will often create meanings that weren't intended. In order to communicate clearly, you need to learn how to create clear visual relationships among design elements. We will talk about how you can use the visual design principles of similarity, contrast, structure, relative position, proportion, and other relationships to help users understand your site's content.

PROFESSIONAL PROFILE *Thomas Sherman*

Creating Visual Heirarchies

Creative Director,
New York City

Thomas Sherman studied graphic design and photography at the Center for Creative Studies in Detroit, Michigan, and the Montserrat College of Art in Beverly, Massachusetts.

He started his undergraduate work in 1987 and studied traditional print design. He developed his layout skills, doing lettering and typography by hand. Although he enjoyed print design, halfway through his undergraduate degree, he transferred to a program that was beginning to use the Macintosh computer to do more digital design. As a result, he feels he got the best of both worlds, the traditional graphic arts training and early exposure to interacting with interfaces as part of the design process.

Thomas says that both online and print design are always goal-oriented: they're about designing effective communication and interaction and knowing what outcome you're trying to support as a result of that interaction. For both print and Web design, you need to understand the users' process in order to accommodate it or create value for them. You're trying to meet users halfway. With online design, however, the goals are more multi-dimensional.

Ironically, Thomas found that designing annual reports with a hundred or more pages proved to be excellent preparation for designing large-scale websites. Dealing with such a huge mass of content meant designing a whole information system, thinking about hierarchies of color and typography, structuring a large volume of information, and communicating that structure through visual hierarchies of interest. He learned to think about and create the rules that describe and define the world of information with which users would interact. This approach to design translated well to creating interfaces, which involves setting up a world for users to interact with that must be consistent and predictable.

According to Thomas, an effective website is one that users don't have to think about to use. Users shouldn't have to work to decipher the nomenclature or to figure out the website's conventions, nor should they have to struggle to accomplish tasks. It's the design's job to resolve all of that. For Thomas, apple.com is a great example of effective Web design on many counts. The site has lots of rich content, but it looks simple and is visually attractive. The horizontal navigation is clear and easy to use, and within a particular product, the subnavigation modules work intuitively and

continued on next page

effectively. The site uses typography really well both to create hierarchy and to make content stand out, and the interaction design makes it really easy to look for software, get an upgrade, or view movie trailers. The site is both usable and enjoyable.

He points out that really good designers learn to create communications or interactions that work on many different levels. Good design has to function well and feel good. For example, decisions regarding color have multidimensional effects on the user experience. Color has very important functional uses. Not only is it quite powerful for directing attention, creating hierarchies, and differentiating types of information, but it's also a crucial part of communicating emotion, identity, and brand.

Showing Relationships, Guiding Users Through the Site

In order to show connections among visual elements and to guide users through the site's content, it is important to understand some basic principles about how we as humans interpret what we see and how we map what we see to concepts. The following subsection talks about using psychological principles of visual perception, called gestalt principles (*gestalt* means "whole" in German), to signal logical relationships and hierarchies and to guide readers through the text.

The color and layout of the page should first provide users with an overall sense of the page's structure and focus, including the relation of the parts to the whole. The distinction between main ideas and subordinate ideas or details should be obvious. Then the design should prompt users to move through the page's content in a particular order. Use the following principles to visually group related items and to avoid inadvertently grouping items that are not related.

Visual Grouping—Gestalt Principles

Visual grouping should communicate relationships and hierarchies. That means users should be able to tell just by looking at the screen which elements are related to one another and which elements or groups of elements are the most important. Visual grouping can affect the order in which readers pay attention to things.

Gestalt Theory

Gestalt theory was developed by a group of German psychologists in the early part of the twentieth century. They studied how the properties of visual elements shape our perceptions, paying particular attention to how we group individual elements into gestalts, or wholes.

As humans, we tend to perceive objects as related to one another if they exhibit the principles of **similarity, proximity,** or **continuity**—that is, if they visually resemble one another (in color or shape, for example), or if they are close together, or if they are continuous (they touch one another or are connected by a line).

Similarity

Elements that are similar in shape, size, color, or orientation will be associated more strongly than items that are not similar. Thus, in Figure 4.3, we associate the white circles as a group, the black circles as a group, and the orange circles as a group.

Notice that the color contrast is even stronger than the association based on shape. Color is a very powerful marker of similarity. See the accompanying feature on color for important guidelines on using color in your screen design, and see Figure 4.4 for an example of a website that uses color to group information items.

The gestalt principle of similarity is also what allows us to recognize differences, making visual contrast a powerful tool for communicating hierarchical relationships. Sharp contrasts draw viewers' attention. Some designers insist that contrast may be the most important element of visual design. In your design, you can use the following contrasts: large/small, light/dark, horizontal/vertical, square/round, smooth/rough, closed/open, colored/plain.

For your visual design drafts, decide which content elements should be visually similar, in order to help users see connections. For example, navigational elements should use visual similarities to reinforce their similar functions. Decide which hierarchical relationships among content elements must be represented, and experiment with ways to show that hierarchy. You'll need to balance the principles of similarity and contrast to show both relationship and hierarchy effectively. And in the next subsection, we discuss how to use the position of your content items to communicate relationship and hierarchy.

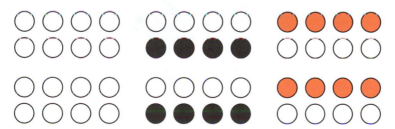

FIGURE 4.3   Similarity and Grouping   These dots are separated into three groups spatially. They are also separated into three groups by their color—white, black, and orange.

Proximity

We associate elements that are close together more strongly than we associate elements that are farther away. Thus, in Figure 4.3, we perceive the eight circles on the left, in the middle, and on the right as groups. Moreover, we see each row of circles as a subgroup, and we perceive the two rows on the top and the two rows on the bottom as subgroups, because of the separation between the second and

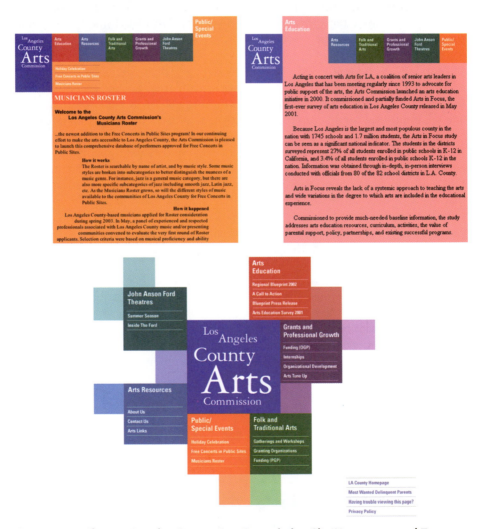

FIGURE 4.4   The Los Angeles County Arts Commission Site Homepage and Two Content Pages   The site uses color to visually group and identify its content areas. Note that users' location within the site is also signaled by the enlarged tab at the top.

third rows. Notice, however, that the strong color contrast between the white, black, and orange circles tends to override the association based on proximity.

Proximity exists at several levels. Elements can be close together or touch or overlap. Or elements can be enclosed in a larger shape or border, as shown in Figure 4.4.

Alignment also affects our perception of proximity and contributes to our sense of the connection among elements. Figure 4.5 provides an example of effective use of proximity and alignment to group content.

Alignment helps organize your content and contributes to the **unity** and **balance** of your layout (discussed in a later subsection). Lines of alignment can sometimes create paths to guide users through the page. The strongest form of alignment is edge alignment, in which the edges of similarly shaped or similarly sized objects are aligned along a clear vertical, horizontal, or diagonal line. Skilled designers can also use center alignment effectively, but novices should probably stick to edge alignment.

As you place your page elements, be aware of the associations you are implying to readers. You want to indicate relationships; you do not want your

FIGURE 4.5   Effective Use of Alignment, Proximity, and Enclosure to Signal Content Groups   This is also an effective example of designing on a grid—note the strong columns. The width of each element is its horizontal space; its height is its vertical space.

Color

Color is a powerful tool for visual differentiation. You can use color to brand, to create hierarchy, to support navigation, and to create a sense of space. Think about color regions as you design the site. You can use color to signal categories, to differentiate information, and to highlight information.

Color is often impractical in printed documents because of its high cost. But color is free in online documents, so you can use it to make your design more attractive, friendlier, and easier to comprehend. You can use color to create emphasis, to make images look better and easier to interpret, and to help mark the function of particular page elements.

As humans, we have powerful emotional reactions to color (see "Emotional Characteristics of Colors," below). Pastel shades are soothing and may soften a message. Vibrant colors can be used to emphasize a point. The stark contrasts in a black-and-white design can be used to create impact and energy.

To some degree, our reactions to color are unique and quite subjective, reflecting our individual experiences and memories. But marketing research shows that cultural groups typically share some color preferences. For example, American consumers associate soft pinks with romance and nostalgia. Color preferences are shaped by individual factors, lifestyle, gender, age, and current fashion.

However, make sure you don't use color alone to convey crucial information. Some users are colorblind; others may have low-end monitors (even monochrome monitors). Color should never be the only clue to meaning; it should supplement and reinforce, not replace, labels or explanations. Make sure the colors you choose are distinguishable on low-end monitors as well as on both PCs and Macs.

Also, be aware that the background color you use will affect viewers' perception of the colors in the foreground. Colors may look more intense on a dark background or washed out on a light background. Reduced color contrast may lessen the impact of your design elements.

You should also be wary of overusing color. Too many different colors can make the screen visually or conceptually overwhelming.

Nielsen (1993, 119) suggests using five to seven colors at most in your coding scheme.

Design Tips

Create a master color chart for your site. For easy reference in the future, put all colors in one file or chart that specifies the **hue, value,** and **saturation** for each color element in your design. (See "Technical Characteristics of Color," below, for definitions of these terms.) You'll need to include a color palette in the *style guide* for your site. To keep your color choices compatible, use color families—shades of gray, pastels, primary colors, earth tones, and so forth. Consider using colors of the same intensity. Make sure you're not letting decorative color draw attention to unimportant information, such as borders and annotations. Instead, use color to differentiate, to connect, to focus attention, and to speed up searching.

Technical Characteristics of Color

- **Hue:** the technical term for what we normally call color. Red, yellow, violet, teal, and so on are all hues.

- **Value:** the lightness or darkness of a color—for example, in the difference between a light brown and a dark brown. Value is affected by adding white or black to a hue.

- **Saturation:** the purity or intensity of a color. Adding gray or the complement of a color (adding green to red, for example) will reduce the intensity of the color. (Many designers complain that the palette of browser-safe colors contains many oversaturated colors.)

Emotional Characteristics of Colors

Warm colors such as red, orange, and yellow advance on the page; cool colors such as blue, green, and purple recede.

- *Red:* a color that stimulates the nervous system and can symbolize energy, passion, or even aggression

- *Orange:* a happy, festive color

- *Blue:* a soothing and relaxing color that can symbolize stability and tradition
- *Purple:* a color that can symbolize strength, daring, and free-spiritedness
- *Violet:* a color that combines the energy of red and the calm of blue and can create a sense of intimacy

- *Yellow:* a color that is stimulating (like red) and warm, and that can suggest energy, sunshine, health, and cheerfulness
- *Green:* a cool, soothing color that can symbolize growth, nature, cleanliness, or even safety

page elements competing with one another for viewers' attention. One of the best ways to indicate relationships is to design your layout using a **grid**—a clear pattern of horizontal and vertical lines—to plan the alignment and visual grouping of your page elements. You also want to pay careful attention to how the **blank space** (generally called white space in print design) between content items supports your information design. See the "Layout" subsection, below, for further discussion of using a grid and blank space in your page designs.

Continuity

Gestalt psychologists also found that, as humans, we prefer continuous, unbroken lines. In fact, we prefer them so much that, if necessary, we will mentally supply the missing pieces of a line ourselves in order to perceive a figure as "complete," as in Figure 4.6. Designers have found that eliciting viewers' active participation to complete a figure can increase the energy and impact of a design. Of course, if you make viewers work too hard, they may well lose interest.

You can also use visual continuity to guide users' eyes through the page. You can employ a particular design element to encourage movement of users' attention in a particular direction. You can then place the next content item that users should see close by and in the same direction as users' eyes are already moving. For example, see Figure 4.7. Most people will find their attention drawn first to the colored circles and then down the curved line to the name "Jacqueline Jones Design."

The principle of continuity also explains why page elements connected by a line are generally perceived as a unit or a group. Items within a border or within a shaded area will tend to be perceived as a group, as in the boxes in Figure 4.5. Thus, as you plan your paper prototypes, you can reinforce your visual groupings by enclosing items in a shaded area of your design grid. You should also be aware that as part of our human preference for seeing things as complete or connected, we tend to interpret figures as simple rather than complex. For example, we would rather see Figure 4.8 as two overlapping triangles than as three distinct figures.

Figure/Ground   The principle of continuity plays an important role in our perception of which elements of the design are "onstage," so to speak, and which are simply part of the "scenery." As humans, we normally divide the visual field

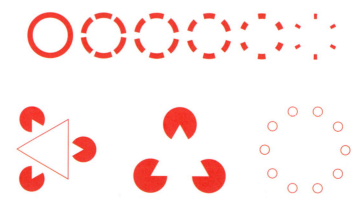

FIGURE 4.6   Examples of Continuity   We perceive the top row of figures as circles, even when the lines are not continuous. In the bottom two figures, we perceive the blank space as triangles, even though no overt lines exist. Similarly, we see the last figure on the bottom row as a circle even though no overt lines connect the smaller circles.

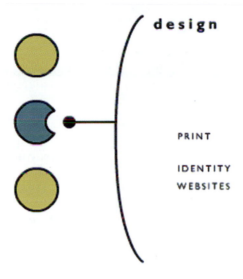

FIGURE 4.7   Visual hierarchy and direction lead viewers' eyes from the colored dots down to the company's name and up to the label "design." The short horizontal line leads users' eyes from the circles to the text on the right.

into two parts: the figure and the ground. The figure is the focus of our attention and is seen as a whole, continuously bounded by a contour or an edge. The ground, or background, is usually at the margin of our attention and is assumed to be behind the figure and to continue behind the figure. If two areas overlap, the smaller area is usually interpreted as the figure, whereas the larger area is usually perceived as the ground.

Be aware that the characteristics of the background will affect viewers' perception of the figure. The color or size or shape of a figure can appear to be different depending on its surroundings.

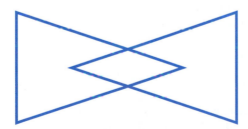

FIGURE 4.8   Interpreting Figures as Simple Rather Than Complex

Designing Content Elements

Now that you have an understanding of some of the visual design principles that need to undergird your design, we'll talk about content elements that require special attention, such as navigational elements, graphics, photographs, and typography.

Navigational Elements

In the last chapter, about designing the user experience, you worked on making your links and headings and other content labels user-centered. You tried to match the site's structure as naturally and intuitively as possible to the structure and flow of users' tasks. Now it's time to use the visual design and placement of the navigational elements to make them easily and intuitively recognizable. Your visual design of navigational elements should contribute to making movement from screen to screen as natural as possible.

Users hate to feel lost. The placement and style of your navigational elements are how you communicate the navigational structure of your site to users. These visual clues about navigation help users know where they are, how they got there, and where they can go next. Consistent placement, weight, behavior, and appearance of navigational elements can help make navigation through the site more intuitive. The visual design of your navigation must signal clearly to users what is selectable and what is selected. The visual design of navigational elements is integral to making your site architecture work.

If you use icons for your navigation, make sure to label them. Icons can be visually easy for users to find, once they know what to look for, but users who are new to the site almost always need labels in order to recognize icons as links and to feel confident that they understand what the icons represent. If there are conventions that users are likely to recognize already, you may want to follow those conventions.

Placement of navigational elements is central to user success. One common strategy is to put global navigation along the top and local navigation along the left margin. In fact, this is so common that users have come to expect this convention, which makes it fairly easy for them to use.

Be careful about embedding links in paragraphs of text or in images. Although embedded links can sometimes be appropriate, usable, helpful, and clear, users can also find embedded links confusing and distracting. Louis Rosenfeld and Peter Morville (1998) suggest using links embedded in paragraphs for nonessential points of interest. Most links should be pulled out into separate lines, to facilitate scanning.

Graphics

Graphics are both a way to communicate information and a way to contribute to the visual look and feel of your site. We discuss informational graphics in more detail in the next chapter, "Creating Effective Content for the Web." Here, we discuss images that you are using primarily for impact or reinforcement. Be careful, however, to keep decorative graphics to a minimum: although they may add interest, they can also be distracting, and they always increase load times. Content graphics provide a higher communication payoff than elements that are simply decorative. See the accompanying feature for tips on when to include an image, possible sources for images, and copyright issues to consider.

Using Photographs Effectively

When using photographs on your webpages, you'll need to think about cropping, size, placement, and framing. You'll also want to consider whether your

---

Checklist for Including a Photograph

Deciding Whether a Photograph Is Worth Including

- The image tells a story and is relevant to the text.
- The image will get readers' attention.
- The image is clear and sharp and looks good.
- The image has been well cropped and will download quickly.
- You have *permission* to use the image.

Sources for Images

- Take your own photos or create an illustration.
- Hire a professional photographer or illustrator.
- Buy from a stock photo agency (make sure you know what rights you are buying).
- Use clip art, if you have permission to do so.
- Customize clip art using a computer drawing program.
- Create an informational graphic (like a table or chart).
- Find public-domain images from old books and magazines.
- Play with typographical elements.

Copyright Issues

The copyright owner has the exclusive right to display a work publicly or to make or distribute copies of the work.

Ideas cannot be copyrighted, but the expression of an idea in words, images, or other fixed form can be copyrighted, even if the work has not yet been published.

In order to use someone else's copyrighted words, images, or music on your website, you will need legal permission from the person who holds the copyright.

Exceptions: Public Domain and Fair Use

You can use works that are in the public domain (the copyright has expired, or the work was produced by a U.S. government agency).

You can also use some copyrighted materials without permission for educational, charitable, or religious purposes. The source must always be specified, and often you can only use part of the work.

final images are balanced, just as you have been trying to keep your overall page layout balanced. Consistent photographic style and lighting can be one tool in keeping your design unified.

    Note: As you apply the following suggestions for editing your images, be sure that you make all your changes to a copy of the image rather than to the original image file. That way, you will always have the original image file to go back to if you want to make a different set of changes. Reediting an already edited image will usually degrade the quality of the image unacceptably. Save the final copy of your photograph for use on your webpage as a .jpg file.

Cropping   First, crop the image to focus viewers' attention on the most essential information. Cropping is a powerful tool for making a weak image into a stronger, more effective one. Eliminate nonessential elements.

    If you have trouble deciding where to crop an image, try printing out the image, then using two L-shaped pieces of paper to cover up the parts of the image that you would crop. Experiment until you find an interesting area of the photograph to keep, as in Figure 4.9. (Note that some image editing software, including Adobe Photoshop, now allows you to simulate this activity by temporarily graying out areas of the image that would be deleted by a crop.)

Sizing   Next, reduce the photo to fit appropriately into your planned layout. It's usually unwise to enlarge photos using an image editor, because the image editor will simply take the colored dots, or pixels, comprising the image and spread them out over a larger area. The result is frequently an effect called "pixelation," in which you get blotches of unsightly color in the image.

    Most computer monitors display images at a resolution of 72 pixels per inch, or ppi. Using an image at a resolution of more than 72 ppi will either cause your image to appear larger on the screen than you intended or increase the load time of your page without providing any benefit to the viewer. To prepare your image for Web display, you should use an image editor to change the resolution of your image to 72 ppi. Or, after you know what dimensions you want for the image, rescan it at a resolution that, when displayed at 72 ppi, will result in the dimensions you want. For example, if you have an image that is 2 inches × 2 inches and you want it to take up 1 inch × 1 inch on your screen, then scan it at 36 ppi.

    If you have multiple images on your screen, consider changing the size and shape of particular images, or the vertical and horizontal orientation, in order to provide visual contrast or dynamic tension. If the images need to look visually linked, emphasize their conceptual similarity through consistent size, color, framing, or placement.

Placing   As you decide where to put your image on the screen, make sure that the action of the photograph will lead readers' eyes into the rest of the screen's content. Face the photograph in the direction you want readers' eyes to go, as in the first example in Figure 4.10.

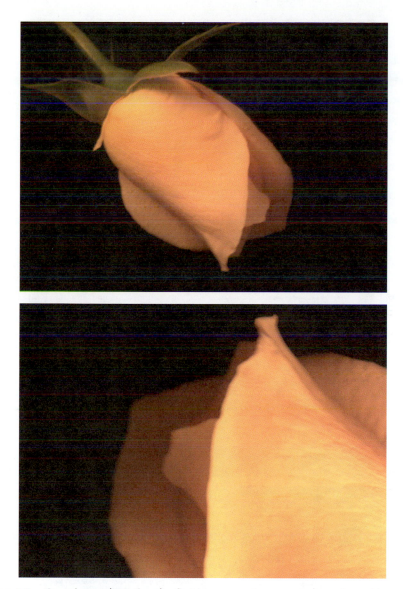

FIGURE 4.9 Cropping and rotating the first image creates a more dramatic and intriguing image, as seen in the second photograph.

Framing   If the image needs to be strongly differentiated from the text, you can add a frame to define the edges. Just make sure that the weight of the frame line is consistent with the rest of your visual design and that it does not overwhelm the image.

Outdoor Adventure Club

Welcome to the Outdoor Adventure Club. OAC is a year round organization that includes people of all skill levels from beginner to expert. We are a diverse group with members of all ages and experience. Being a member of OAC is a great way to introduce yourself to new, exciting experiences that otherwise might be intimidating or overwhelming.

Learn to rock climb, roll a kayak, bike in Nova Scotia - the possibilities are limitless. If you already have a specific expertise, share your knowledge with others who appreciate anything you may have to contribute.

Club Info I What's New I Event Calendar I List Serve I Checklists
Bulletin Board I Photos I Trip Stories I Links I Classifieds I Guest Book

FIGURE 4.10 The top design has clear direction; in the lower designs, however, the photos do not clearly lead viewers into the text.

Typography—Visual Design of Text

When readers look at the text on your screen, they will be affected by the mood or visual tone of the text, by its density, by its legibility, and by the contrast among parts of the text. Of course, they will also be affected by their own prior attitudes or beliefs about the subject matter as well as by the context and the urgency of their need for the information you're providing.

The style, shape, and size of your letters, and the spaces between letters and between words, will either reinforce or impede your efforts to communicate with users. These visual attributes of the text are called typography. The typographical choices you make while designing your pages are essential to communicating with users and are a big factor in how your pages will look. You want a typestyle that will be legible, support your site's overall look and feel, provide visual clues about meaning, and guide users through the information.

Your choice of typestyle plays an integral role in creating the mood and tone of your site. Are you trying to be hip? Playful? Serious? Elegant? The typestyle can help you. But don't sacrifice legibility for mood or artistic effect. Users will hardly feel welcome if your site's content is hard to read. And be wary of using more than two typestyles in your visual design: you'll reduce the visual coherence of your site. If you want to create visual emphasis for selected text elements, try changing the size or the weight of the type (making it bold, for example). Readers notice changes in the size or weight (bolding) of the type more than they notice changes in typeface. (Note that to get a cleaner look, designers prefer to use a heavyweight typeface in the same family as the body text rather than apply a "bold" effect to a regular-weight typeface.)

Unfortunately, choosing a typestyle for the Web is a bit trickier than choosing a typestyle for a print document. In print, the style you choose is the style readers will see. On the Web, if the user's computer doesn't have your chosen font installed, the browser will default to another font. (The accompanying feature suggests some typefaces that work well for different platforms.) You can control the appearance of your text by displaying your text as a graphic, but that dramatically slows down the loading of your pages and is usually unacceptable. Although you may sometimes choose to display page banners and logos as graphics, in the real world of slow Web access, you can't display the entire page content as a graphic. So you will probably want to specify one or two alternate fonts, with at least one widely available option, to keep the display that users will actually see as predictable as possible. And make sure you preview your

Typefaces That Are Roughly Equivalent for Different Platforms			
	Windows	**Macintosh**	**Unix**
Proportional, Web	Verdana	Geneva	—
Proportional, print	Arial	Helvetica	Helvetica
Proportional, print	Times	Times New Roman	Times
Fixed-width	Courier	Courier New	Courier

pages with different browsers and on different platforms to get a sense of how well the design survives in various environments.

Text Design Suggestions

Studies show that reading online takes 20 percent to 40 percent longer than reading on paper. Since Web users are more than ready to click away to another site, you need to work hard to make your text easy and enjoyable to read. Users will appreciate a large, legible typestyle with clean lines. See the accompanying feature "Suggestions for Making Online Text More Legible" for additional ideas.

You can emphasize headings by using bold type and a larger type size. Adding a rule can also make headlines stand out, but overuse of horizontal rules can mark your visual design as amateur. You can also emphasize headings by adding a shaded background or by using reverse type—light type on a dark background. But be aware that dark backgrounds make white text look smaller and thinner, so if you're displaying white text on a dark background, you'll need to use a heavier weight font and wider-than-normal letter spacing.

As you make decisions about the visual appearance of your text, you will probably need to design the following textual elements:

- Body text
- Titles and headings
- Tables, lists, and captions
- Links

For each of these elements, choose a typeface, a size, and a weight (normal, bold, extra black). Choose a grammatical structure you will use to maintain parallelism.

Remember that the primary focus of your document design is to communicate the structure of the text and the role of particular text elements—their purpose, their relationship to one another. The style, size, **leading** (a measurement of the distance between lines of text), and line length of your text can help communicate your argument by indicating the role of a particular text element. Typography can also indicate the importance of a particular text element to the argument, signaling that some text elements are main points while clearly signaling that other elements are subordinate to the body text. For example, you want the visual appearance of mouseovers, pop-up windows, captions, references, and links to be different from the appearance of content text, and you want headings to look clearly different from body text. (One common form of technical communication through the Web is delivering online help or technical support information. See the accompanying feature for some suggestions on planning the visual design of this type of information.)

Finally, remember that all your decisions about type should be clearly explained and demonstrated in your style guide, so that future additions to the site

Suggestions for Making Online Text More Legible

Use a Sans-Serif Typeface

Typefaces are broadly grouped into serif and sans-serif categories. Serifs are the little tails that appear on the ends of letters in some typefaces—such as the typeface of this sentence. In contrast, this sentence is in Verdana, which is a sans-serif font, with no little tails. Research indicates that sans-serif fonts are normally easier to read online—probably because screen resolution is lower than print resolution, so typefaces with simpler, cleaner outlines are more legible.

Use a Larger Type Size Than in Print Documents

Style sheets allow designers to specify type sizes, but you can make your site more accessible for visually impaired users by specifying your font size as a percentage of the browser default rather than as an absolute number of pixels. That way, users can still choose to enlarge your text for viewing.

Use Relatively Short Line Lengths

According to Karen Schriver (1997), a noted researcher on document design, paper documents can get away with forty to seventy characters per line, or forty to sixty characters for sans-serif typefaces, but online documents should use line lengths of thirty to fifty characters.

Use Ragged-Right Margins for Body Text for Western Audiences

Using a ragged-right margin means not justifying the text on the right margin. Text that is justified on both sides can be hard to read even in print documents, because justification can cause excessive hyphenation of words. It can also create accidental rivers of white space caused by unpredictable variations in spacing between words. These rivers pull the eye downward, making reading more difficult. These problems are exacerbated in online documents. For audiences that normally read right to left, the right margin should be justified and the left margin should be ragged.

Avoid Putting Text in All Capital Letters

Text that is entirely in capital letters is harder to read, because all the words have basically the same shape—a rectangle.

Avoid Excessive Use of Italics

Italic text is harder to read than normal text even in a print document. On screen, italic text often reproduces especially poorly. However, you should italicize titles rather than underlining them. On the Web, users typically assume that underlined terms are links.

Use Plenty of Blank Space Around Text

Use blank space around paragraphs and columns to improve legibility. Text with lots of surrounding blank space may attract and hold readers' attention longer. According to Schriver (1997), a good rule of thumb is that your text should occupy about 40 percent to 50 percent of the screen.

can be made visually consistent. This is particularly important if you're working on a group project. Putting in a little extra time at this design stage can save a lot of time later when you have to go back and edit the site for consistency. Creating a style sheet for your website that all the pages can reference will help (see the website accompanying this text for an introduction to style sheets).

Layout

As you design your page layout, your goal is to use the placement of content items to suggest to users how to make sense of your content and to guide them as they scan the screen. You want to use the layout to prompt users to see the material as organized and related and to help them identify what is important. The layout communicates the logical structure of your content. It helps users to grasp the big picture—to see how the parts relate to the whole.

Designing on a Grid

Many designers use a grid to guide their layout design, as in Figure 4.11. A grid can provide continuity among diverse pages. The grid guides the placement of major page elements. It can also help you communicate hierarchy;

Delivering Help or Support Information Online

If you are writing help screens or support information, you need to think carefully about the visual design of hints, notes, cautions, text that represents user input, and text that represents computer output. Provide a strong visual signal that separates steps to be followed by users from explanations, in order to make the instructions easy to find and follow.

To plan the layout of your page, you must carefully consider the context in which your instructions will be used. Will users print them out, or will they need to see two screens at once?

Users are also likely to access your screens in unpredictable order, so the first text on each screen must clearly identify the information that is available on that screen. Help users find out immediately whether they have the information they need.

Universities and businesses know that delivering support via the Web is much cheaper than passing out information to users one phone call at a time. But Web-delivered support will only be effective if users feel comfortable and helped.

you may isolate some elements, to emphasize their importance, and show other elements as subordinate. At the same time, you use the grid to plan your representation of how content is grouped together into chunks. When looking at your screen, users must be able to grasp the logic behind the organization of your content, find the specific information they need, and then interpret the information once they find it.

Obviously, if your content is not organized or logical or clearly visualized, using a grid won't make it any clearer to readers. But you can use the grid to help clarify your organization and visualization, and the process of designing the grid can help you spot problems in your thinking that need to be resolved.

Remember that you're designing screens, not pages. Screens are wider than they are tall, whereas standard letter-size paper is taller than it is wide. As you define your grid and begin to create your paper prototypes, you'll want to design using a landscape orientation. Normally, you want to avoid long lines of text that go across the screen, so instead, you may consider making sections of the screen into sidebars for summaries, navigation information, and so forth. You can take advantage of the landscape orientation to add design elements that wouldn't work as well on paper.

FIGURE 4.11   The underlying grid shared by the BBC section page and the content page creates visual consistency.

You should probably do your paper drafting on a screen print of an empty browser window. This will help you keep the environment concrete and clearly in mind. It will also help you ensure that important screen elements appear "above the fold," or above the scroll line. A few studies have indicated that some users don't scroll and thus miss content that doesn't appear above the scroll line. Note that the position of the scroll line will vary depending on the screen resolution of the monitor. See the accompanying feature for some standard screen sizes.

Be aware that window sizes are going to vary and that users can choose to resize their browser windows anytime they want. Your design must be able to withstand a dynamic display environment. But this dynamic environment is an opportunity as well as a challenge; Web designers need to find ways to create designs that can accommodate a certain amount of change in display size. Ideally, you'll want a layout that will accommodate some degree of change in size, down to a minimum size that preserves readability.

Standard Screen Sizes

800 × 600 pixels

1,024 × 768 pixels

1,280 × 1,024 pixels

1,600 × 1,200 pixels

As you design your grid, plan the size and pixels of your content elements so that key content is "above the fold."

The safest method for ensuring that your design will be visible is to change your screen resolution to 1024 × 768 while you design.

Using the grid, plan your horizontal and vertical space so that it supports and communicates your content. Vertical space is the vertical size of screen elements and the vertical distance between elements. Horizontal space is the horizontal width of elements and the horizontal distance between elements. Indentation is an example of horizontal space. Horizontal and vertical space can signal parallel text elements and grouping, and it can set one element off from another.

Stick to dramatic horizontal cues. It's easy for horizontal spacing to look accidental and messy instead of deliberate (see Figures 4.12 and 4.13). This is a common problem in student resumés: too many lines of indentation or horizontal alignment make the resumés look choppy and ragged, even chaotic. Rather than overuse horizontal cues, use principles of grouping and continuation to reflect rhetorical and logical groupings, to guide users through the screen.

Clear, consistent horizontal and vertical lines in the screen layout provide visual stability. Diagonal lines create dynamic tension.

Using Blank Space Effectively

As you design your grid, make sure that you use adequate amounts of blank space and that you arrange it effectively. For print documents, you would typically design the page to have 50 percent text and 50 percent blank space. For

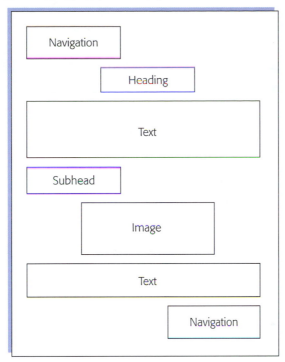

FIGURE 4.12   Haphazard horizontal spacing makes your content visually confusing.

screens, however, you need to make the text noticeably less dense. Karen Schriver (1997) suggests using 30 percent to 40 percent text, with the rest being blank space. But remember that it's the placement and shape of the blank space that matter most, not its amount. Blank space can be active or passive; it can play an informational role, or it can just frame information. It can simply provide a valuable rest for the eye and brain, or it can actively direct the eye through the layout, showing connections, progression, or emphasis.

Blank space is a powerful tool for signaling the document's logical and rhetorical structure. These cues organize readers' perception and shape their interpretation of what they see and read. Effective spatial cues help communicate the structure of your message visually; they help readers make good judgments about data.

Finally, be aware that although grids are good for designing rectangular information spaces, they are not the only way to approach spatial design. Many ads or works of art use triangles or even circles as their organizing principle. These alternatives may sometimes be appropriate, especially for introductory pages that need to be more eye-catching.

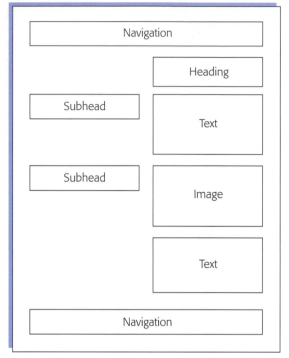

FIGURE 4.13   Even a simple grid can make your content much more accessible.

Maintaining Visual Balance—Symmetry and Asymmetry

The material on your screen designs must be visually balanced. That means you need to balance the size and position of the elements on the page. You also have to pay attention to the balance of light and dark and the balance between content space and blank space. Balancing these design elements doesn't necessarily mean that they are present in equal proportions; on the contrary, as we discussed previously, contrast provides emphasis, communicates difference, and adds drama or impact. You can use contrasts between large and small, dark and light, and different colors as well as contrasts involving position. But even your contrasts need to provide a sense of balance in the design.

The easiest form of balance is symmetry, and student Web designers sometimes overuse this technique. Page layouts don't need to be symmetrical in order to be balanced, however. Balance means that the visual weight and distance from the center of elements on each side of your balance point are roughly equal. That means that a smaller visual element that is farther from the balance point can balance a larger visual element that is close to the balance point. Thus, you can choose to have a symmetrical design with a diagonal axis of symmetry rather than a vertical axis of symmetry, as in Figure 4.14, or you can pursue visual balance with an asymmetrical design, as in Figure 4.15.

Asymmetry can sometimes look more dynamic and energetic and less formal than symmetry. In order to maintain the balance of your design, though, violations of symmetry need to be pronounced enough to look deliberate. Marginal violations of symmetry will probably look awkward and merely disrupt the balance of the page.

Evaluating the Success of Your Design

One way to train yourself to pay attention to the relationships among the visual elements on your page is to use the "squint test." By half-closing one eye, you can get a sense for the major shapes, colors, sizes, and positions of the visual elements in your design. You can also use this method to look at how the "accidental" shapes created by the blank space around the content elements of the design interact with one another.

Use the squint test to identify the visual focal point of the screen, the point that gets viewers' immediate attention. Does the focal point encourage readers' interest in the rest of the page content?

To guide users' attention through the content on your page, you usually want to establish a point of visual dominance, where users' eyes will be drawn first. Then you'll use the principles of proximity, continuity, similarity, and contrast described above to guide users' eyes through the rest of your content.

Also use the squint test to evaluate the balance and proportion of the page elements. Remember that every element in the visual field interacts with other elements. That's why it's so important to plan the major elements of the layout as early as possible. The appearance of a figure (especially its apparent size, color, and shape) depends on where it is and what's around it. Making changes

FIGURE 4.14   Note the diagonal axis of symmetry in this section of a portfolio page.

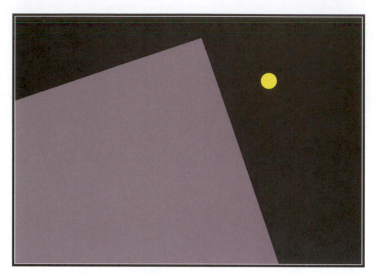

FIGURE 4.15   Asymmetrical Balance

at the last minute, without leaving time to evaluate the effect on the overall design, really can ruin the whole layout. So plan ahead and allow time to test and revise your designs.

Designing the Homepage

The homepage is crucial for keeping visitors on the site long enough to discover the site's usefulness. The primary purpose of this page, which should load especially quickly, is to demonstrate how the site is relevant to users' needs and goals. You must immediately persuade users that they want to stay on the site, that the site will be useful or interesting to them.

This page also bears the burden of establishing the site's credibility and quality and of making users feel welcome. It sets the mood, look, and feel of the site. The homepage should communicate what kind of site you've created and make the site's structure apparent (see Figure 4.16). Your visual design and your navigational elements should invite users to navigate the site in certain ways. And your visual design will provide clues for users about what your design team thought was important.

Only the most important information should be included on the homepage: an introduction to and summary of the site's content, an introduction to the site's navigational structure, and a clear path to all of the site's important functionality. There is always pressure to cram more onto the homepage. Choose what you include on your homepage designs very carefully—and make sure the most essential content is above the fold.

FIGURE 4.16   An effective homepage design communicates a site's purpose and structure and also sets the mood. The homepage should invite users into the site's content.

Capturing Design Decisions in a Style Guide

Producing effective documentation for those who have to build, maintain, or add to your site is just as important as creating an effective design in the first place. A style guide is a document to which editors, graphic designers, and engineers can refer to help them understand and maintain the look and feel of the site. It must be long enough to be detailed but short enough that people will (1) read it and (2) follow it.

A style guide is usually an interesting balance of overall general description and painstaking detail. A typical guide will have page templates that show pixel measurements for navigation and other page-layout elements. It will also contain paragraphs that attempt to describe the overall mood and tone of the design. Style guides are often posted on a private password-protected server, so that different user groups—such as engineers, illustrators, or content providers—can navigate easily to the particular section that matters to them. The sections of your style guide will vary depending on your project, but here are some typical ones:

- *Audience:* Help future contributors to the site to know the site's users by including photos, persona information, and demographic information.

- *Tone:* As you gathered requirements, you chose three adjectives to capture the essence of your site—for example, authoritative, professional, commanding. You want future additions to the site, as well as marketing materials that are produced to attract people to the site, to extend the tone of the site and brand, so a good style guide can make it easy for advertising agencies to partner with you or your client. Present specific examples of the types of language you want them to use. Explain the brand attributes you've identified, so that content producers will understand the story they are trying to tell through both the language and the visual design of the site.

- *Editorial consistency:* Specify punctuation, capitalization, client trademarks and product names, styles for links, footers, lists, and every other textual element. You can also include an annotated list of stylebooks, dictionaries, and other reference works. This section will help client, third-party, and freelance authors, editors, and proofreaders.

- *Graphic and multimedia consistency:* Be as specific as possible about the size, color, and placement of content items that need to stay consistent. If you are using sounds to accompany actions, then specify usage, volume levels, sampling rates, and so on. Set standards for any video files or other multimedia elements.

- *Functionality:* Specify any input/output controls, error-handling rules and messages, and business rules governing site transactions and functionality (for example, it's illegal to transfer funds from a credit card to a brokerage account).

- *Usability:* Identify the key processes that must be free from usability problems, such as registration, checkout, ticket purchase, or search. Set clear usability standards in your style guide, so that future developers can be held accountable for the usability of their additions to your work.

- *Visual design:* Describe what the main sections of the site should look like with wireframes that show exactly, to scale, the pixel dimensions of each screen element, including identity and logo, advertising, global and secondary navigation, photo areas, text areas, and blank space. Ideally, a nondesigner should be able to take your graphic design templates and create pages that look consistent with the rest of the site. Include guidelines about logo/identity rules and photo editorial guidelines. Specify fonts, colors, and so forth. You'll use text, examples, and templates in this section.

- *Production specifications:* Specify server access information, directory structure, file-naming conventions, file formats, production art statistics, and file size limits. This information will document the site and help the client or third party to maintain and update it.

Getting Ready to Test

Your own design can't help but seem obvious to you: not only did you think it up, but you've also been working with it day after day. Of course it looks clear and straightforward! But make sure you test the site with actual users, as discussed in Chapter 6, to see whether your design works for them, and avoid the temptation to blame problems on the users rather than on your design. You can only lose by not making your site friendly and functional for the people who will be using it. If you want to create beautiful designs to be admired rather than used, then you probably are more interested in art for art's sake rather than the applied art of visual design for the Web.

Making sense of a website involves a collaboration between designers and users. It's both an individual act of reading and making meaning and enjoyment and a communal act enabled by shared beliefs, shared conventions, shared language, and shared culture. The most you can hope to do as a designer is to shape the meanings interpreted/constructed by users. What they understand from your material is a product of what they read, the order in which they read it, and what the users bring to the text themselves in terms of their values, attitudes, beliefs, knowledge, and culture. Each user's background will be somewhat different, and each user may choose to interact with the content of your site in a different order. No one can control meaning and interpretation; the most we can do is to use words, pictures, layout, and other design cues to shape meaning and guide users through the site's content.

✔ FINAL CHECKLIST

Homepage

- At first glance, does your site look inviting, professional, and easy to use?
- Does the homepage communicate what kind of site you've created?
- Does the homepage navigation communicate the major sections of the site?
- Does the homepage avoid the need to scroll, even on an 800 × 600 pixel screen?
- Does the homepage load quickly?

General Questions

- Is the functionality of your site easy to find?
- Is the navigation easy to find and visually consistent?
- Does your site have a consistent visual mood and tone? Does each page look like part of your site?
- Have you used images, color, and placement to emphasize important content?
- Does each design element contribute effectively to your message? Are there any design elements that you could eliminate or simplify to make your design more straightforward visually?

Photographs

- Are your photographs cropped to focus users' attention on essential information?
- Have you sized your photographs to fit appropriately into your layout? Has the resolution of your image been set to 72 pixels per inch?
- Have you standardized your sizes, compression settings, and naming conventions for all images?

Multimedia

- If you are using sounds, have you defined volume levels, sampling rates, and sounds to accompany actions?

Typography

- Have you chosen a typeface that will be legible onscreen?
- Does the typeface help to create the right mood and tone for your site?
- Is your type size large enough? Have you made it possible for visually impaired users to enlarge your text so it will be easier to read?

- Have you kept line lengths shorter than about fifty characters?
- Do the size, style, and placement of your text elements reinforce the logical relationship among them? Have you created a visual hierarchy that helps communicate your logical hierarchy?

Page Layout

- Do you use your page layout to communicate visually the logical hierarchy of your content items? Does it help users see the relationship between specific content items and the overall content?
- Do you use similarity and placement to show logical relationships effectively?
- Do you use blank space effectively? Do you provide enough blank space? Does your blank space help communicate the structure of your information?
- Is each page visually balanced? Do you have a good balance of light and dark? A good balance between screen areas (top and bottom, left and right)?
- Are users' eyes drawn to a logical starting point on each page?
- Have you placed your images so that they lead users' eyes into the rest of the screen's content?
- Does your page design look open and inviting rather than cramped, busy, or intimidating?

Style Guide

- Have you included screen shots of all major pages?
- Have you made your users concrete through personas or task scenarios?
- Have you provided demographic information about your major user groups?
- Have you described the site's tone and mood?
- Have you described the branding characteristics and goals of the site?
- Have you specified placement, size, and color of content items that need to stay consistent, such as logos, advertising, navigation, photo areas, text areas, and blank space? Have you included examples?
- Have you defined specific usability goals for key aspects of your site?
- Have you specified inputs, outputs, and controls for all functionality?

REFERENCES

Bringhurst, Robert. 1997. *Elements of Typographic Style.* 2d ed. Roberts, Wash.: Hartley and Marks.

Davis, Jack, and Susan Merritt. 1998. *The Web Design WOW! Book.* New York: Peach-Pit Press.

Kostelnick, Charles, and David D. Roberts. 1997. *Designing Visual Language: Strategies for Professional Communicators.* New York: Allyn & Bacon.

Mullet, Kevin, and Darrell Sano. 1995. *Designing Visual Interfaces: Communication-Oriented Techniques.* Englewood Cliffs, N.J.: SunSoft Press.

Nielsen, Jakob. 1993. *Usability Engineering.* New York: Morgan Kaufmann.

Rosenfeld, Louis, and Peter Morville. 1998. *Information Architecture for the World Wide Web.* Sebastopol, CA: O'Reilly.

Schriver, Karen. 1997. *Dynamics in Document Design: Creating Texts for Readers.* New York: Wiley.

Toor, Marcelle Lapow. 1998. *Graphic Design on the Desktop: A Guide for the Non-Designer.* 2d ed. New York: Wiley.

5 Creating Effective Content for the Web

CHAPTER HIGHLIGHTS

Understanding How People Read on the Web
Gathering Content Information
Keeping Your Content User-Focused
  Building a Relationship with Users
  Breaking Content into User-Focused Chunks
Structuring Content Visually
  Keep Your Text Focused and Concise
  Start Content Chunks with Clear Main Points
  Use Strong Verbs and the Active Voice
  Use Lists
  Use Meaningful Headings and Subheadings
  Highlight Key Information
Making the Most of Your Online Environment
  Add Links to Further Information
  Use Scrolling Appropriately
  Use Frames Cautiously, When Appropriate
  Include Informational Images and Graphics
  Use Multimedia Appropriately
  Use Interactivity Appropriately
  Make Content Easy to Find
Establishing Credibility
Keeping Your Communication Ethical
Editing Your Content
Testing Your Content for Effectiveness

One of the exciting challenges of preparing content for the Web is the opportunity to include graphics, sound, video, and animation. However, although it may seem as if the graphics or the animation or the audio provide all the glamour and capture all the attention in website design, most often your text is what really gets the bulk of your information across to users. Thus, much of this chapter focuses on creating effective text for the Web.

You must craft your content very carefully to focus on user needs and goals, and you must pay particular attention to integrating the message of your text with the visual design and layout of your pages. Good writing means figuring out what your users need to know and the order in which they need to know it, and then structuring the information so that it makes sense to them. If you are building the site for a client, part of your job is to help the client figure out what information must be on the site and then to make sure that information gets communicated effectively. You'll be participating in strategic decisions about what information to include and then using the visual structure and emphasis of the page to help organize that information. You need to help users understand what they see when they look at your content, which means you'll have to maintain a user focus in your document design and then ruthlessly adapt that design based on the results of your usability testing (described in Chapter 6).

Your goal is to guide—not force—users through the information in a way that makes their experience useful and enjoyable.

Understanding How People Read on the Web

People typically read text on the Web differently than they read print text. As Jakob Nielsen (1997) has pointed out, people don't really read text on the Web—they scan it. One reason for this is the fact that words on a screen are fuzzy compared to words on paper. A printout from a laser printer has about six hundred dots per inch, whereas the screen has seventy-two or ninety-six dots per inch. It's simply not comfortable to read fuzzy text on a screen that's unpleasantly far away. Naturally, most Web users read with their hand on the mouse ready to bolt at any time.

That means you have to design your text so that scanning it is likely to produce good comprehension and retention. You'll need to keep your content concise, keep line lengths short, use headings and subheadings, and logically organize your page's blank space to reinforce the logical grouping of your content. Your goal is to help users get the information that they most need and that the client most wants them to have.

How users read, and how much time users will be likely to spend with your content, also depends on their purpose in coming to the site. Is users' goal to be entertained? To learn something? To buy something? To answer a specific question? Will users want to focus on parts of the information, or will they want to read the whole thing? Will users focus on different sections at different times? Will they access the information more than once? The answers to these questions will help determine how you break your information into chunks, how you arrange it, and what tone you use—whether to be entertaining, or focused and practical.

Once you've clarified the purpose of your site, it's time to start gathering the content you'll need to support users' goals.

Gathering Content Information

Gathering content information for your site can be a time-consuming process, especially if you are dependent on client personnel from different departments. Some of these people may be motivated to respond to your request for information quickly, but others may see your request as an unwelcome interruption. Compiling the necessary information requires patience and good interpersonal skills.

Your first job is to identify what content information you'll need. Much of this identification should have happened during your user research in Chapter 2, when you generated a list of the tasks that users are going to want to perform. You should also have copious notes on what information users will need in order to perform each task. You can also go back to the "wish lists" of information that client personnel said they'd like to have appear on the site.

Use the information architecture you've already created (see Chapter 3) to produce wireframes that define the content you'll need for each page. Develop user scenarios, then walk through them using paper prototype pages, to help identify the information users will need and want at each point in the process. Keep users clearly in mind: we recommend posting the personas (including a photo) that you created during your user observation above your work area. Ask questions from the users' point of view. Get real user questions if you can, by having users look at and try to use prototype versions of your pages. Use an iterative process; as you acquire and incorporate additional information, walk through your scenarios again to identify any further questions you may need to answer.

One key method for gathering content information is to interview client personnel and **subject-matter experts,** often referred to in technical communication as "SMEs." See the accompanying feature for tips on how to interview client personnel and subject-matter experts effectively.

Your content may also come from print materials provided by your client or from your user research or even from library or online research. But even if the client has print materials that you can use as a content source, you'll need names of client personnel who can double-check accuracy and answer additional questions.

Make sure you don't include information on the website just because you have it. Instead, focus on maintaining an effective balance between user goals and client goals. If your content doesn't contribute to the goals and mission of your site, it will be a liability rather than an asset.

Keeping Your Content User-Focused

One of the most crucial steps in drafting your Web text is identifying which text is most important, based on both client goals and user goals. In order to make your text scannable, as discussed in the next section, you'll need to make sure you emphasize the most important information. You can use the user and client

Interviewing Subject-Matter Experts (SMEs)

An interview is a cooperative exchange of information through words and body language. Your ability to interview well is often crucial to your success in gathering the content information you need.

A successful interview requires advance planning, a certain amount of trust between the interviewer and the interviewee, and some degree of investment in the interview's success on the part of both parties.

Conducting a Successful Interview

Before You Go

- Think about why the subject-matter expert should care about the interview's outcome.

- Show your respect for the SME's expertise. Learn what you can before you come.

- Think about the SME's probable preconceptions. Be aware that this person may feel that time spent with you comes at the expense of other important work.

- Plan the length and location of the interview. Do your best to respect the SME's time.

- Prepare a list of questions, including both open-ended questions that will elicit overview information and explanations, and closed-ended questions that will elicit specific information that you need. Keep your list of questions flexible, but put them in a logical order and make sure they are clearly worded.

During the Interview

- Use the first few minutes to build trust. Show your appreciation for the SME's time and knowledge.

- Concentrate on what you hear, making an effort to listen, understand, and remember.

- Ask questions to reinforce your comprehension and memory.

- Listen for main ideas.

- Restate main points periodically.

- Watch for nonverbal messages.

- Keep your own nonverbal messages positive.

- Provide clear feedback.

- Use the final minutes to say thank you, to summarize, and to confirm any future plans. Ask the SME if there is anything he or she would like to share that hasn't yet been discussed.

After the Interview

- Review your notes carefully and thoroughly, while your memory is fresh, so that you're less likely to need clarification later.

- Keep any promises you made during the interview or about the results of the interview.

- Send a thank-you note, if appropriate. Let the SME's manager know how helpful the interview was, if appropriate.

PROFESSIONAL PROFILE *Catherine Wilson*

From Technical Communicator to Web Professional: Focusing on Ease of Use

Director of Website Development for Pfizer.com

When Catherine Wilson was getting a degree in technical communication at Bowling Green State University, in Ohio, she never dreamed she'd be responsible for the corporate website for the largest pharmaceutical company in the world. But she was laying the groundwork from the beginning. As a student, she talked to working technical communication professionals, asking them what they wished they had studied in school, and based on these interviews, she supplemented her coursework with offset printing, TV production, film production, and other communications media.

She also developed a strong commitment to user research and usability testing. Early in her career, she wrote user manuals for surgical equipment for health-care professionals and service manuals for biomedical engineers. Some of this equipment was so complicated that nurses would tell the surgeons "It's not working today" rather than set it up. She was committed to making the manuals easier to use by working directly with real users and testing the manuals with them.

Her interest in online design began in the 1980s, when she used Hyper-Card and worked on an interactive project for a client. She instantly loved the fact that information no longer had to be vertical, and this piqued her interest in the Internet.

In 1995 and 1996, she assembled a team of people to build a corporate website—on their own time—for a company that was a division of Pfizer. Soon after, she was offered a position on the pfizer.com team.

Now she is director of that team and responsible for a redesign of a corporate website with more than two thousand pages and links to more than three hundred other Pfizer websites. Her ability to set up processes to input and track changes, lead the cross-divisional design team, and manage multiple vendors effectively has never been more crucial. Catherine started the pfizer.com redesign with focus groups and usability testing. The focus groups provided a clear sense of what people want and need when they visit a corporate pharmaceutical website. Usability testing of the old website enabled her to identify its strengths and weaknesses.

With this information, she recommended redesigning the corporate website to balance user needs with business goals and requirements. Her team developed the information architecture, had users respond to flat sample designs,

continued on next page

and then built two interactive prototypes for more involved usability testing. After one design was selected, the site went through additional rounds of usability testing, and it will continue to be tested after it is launched. Catherine suggests that usability testing is like brushing your teeth: just as brushing your teeth is part of your daily routine, user research and usability testing should be part of every Internet initiative throughout its life cycle. Iterative testing and redesign are the key to the major improvements of the redesigned site.

Since the corporate website provides a wide range of information (product, investor, shareholder, and so forth), user task success is particularly crucial. Members of Catherine's team have worked especially hard on the text they use to describe links, looking at the reading level of visitors and spending several rounds of iterative testing on word choice, length, and location on the site. Her team wants to make sure that users can find the information they need quickly.

Catherine is living proof that technical communicators can be valuable contributors to the Web design field. Her advice to students is to push the envelope and to push their own limits until they can do things they never thought possible.

research techniques described in the chapters on designing the user experience and usability testing to prioritize your information so that you can make it truly user-focused and accessible.

You want to write with what Kitty Locker (1999) calls a "you attitude," which means looking at things from the readers' point of view, emphasizing what readers want to know, respecting their abilities and expertise, and protecting their ego. See the accompanying feature for Locker's tips on keeping your text focused on readers rather than on the writer.

Building a Relationship with Users

As you get ready to begin drafting, review what you found out about your users in your early research. What level of knowledge and experience with this material or this kind of site do they already have? What beliefs do they already have about the content of your site? What is their attitude toward your material likely to be? Skeptical? Enthusiastic? Apathetic? Adapt both your language and your content to what you already know about your readers in order to communicate effectively. For example, if your users are likely to be resistant to your message, you may need more examples, and you may need to sound as objective as possible. Too much enthusiasm in describing your offerings (or your client's offerings) may cause readers to discount what you say.

If you are likely to have international users, think about how differences in background or culture might affect their perception of your material.

You should also consider what your relationship to your users is. Is this an intranet site or a site aimed at acquiring and maintaining customers? Are the users your bosses, clients, subordinates, or peers? What kind of relationship are you trying to build with users? What kind of persona will they expect from you? Remember that expectations about persona or about how relationships should be built will vary from culture to culture. And, of course, if you're building this site for a client, you've got to base your writing on the relationship the client wants to build with users.

Breaking Content into User-Focused Chunks

One of the first steps in drafting is to break your content into screen-sized chunks of information. Your goal is to create clear visual patterns that communicate the logical structure of the information to users quickly. Each screen will then be subdivided into smaller chunks of information using headings and subheadings. Ideally, each chunk of text should cover one point and should feel like a logical unit. It should answer one question, about one subject, for one purpose. Writing the question that each chunk is intended to answer on your paper prototypes can help you maintain this focus.

Each chunk should also be tightly organized. Possible organizational structures for your information include using **narrative order,** describing a process or an occurrence through time; or using **logical order,** consisting of an assertion,

---

Maintaining a "You Attitude"

The following valuable suggestions for writing with a "you attitude" are adapted from Kitty Locker (1999):

- Focus on what readers get or can do as a result of your material; stress what readers want to know. Show why information is important to readers, how it will affect them. Explain clearly, logically, and in detail how readers will benefit; use vivid sensory detail or scenarios, if appropriate.

- Arrange information to meet readers' needs, not yours. Use headings and lists to make key information more available, and make sure headings are user-centered. Put the information that readers will be most interested in first.

- Don't talk about your feelings or desires or what you want (unless your motivations and goals are something readers specifically want to know).

- Think carefully about how readers feel or are likely to respond to something. Find out, if possible. Answer any questions readers are likely to have.

- Be complete—but also be sensitive to readers' needs. (For example, you may want to put some information on separate pages, allowing users to link to it if they want.)

Make sure the sentence structure itself reflects this focus on readers; don't let the sentence structure focus on the writer.

Ways to Organize Information

Create Categories That Are

- Topical (subject-based)

- Task-oriented (searching for airline flight information, comparing prices, making flight or hotel reservations, and so forth)

- Audience-specific (for example, university home sites often group information based on who is most likely to want it, with sections for prospective students, current students, faculty, or other employees)

Items Might Be Categorized By

- Geographical location or origin.

- Chronology.

- Alphabetical order.

- Hierarchy (small to large, least expensive to most expensive, order of importance).

- Type, concept, or the like. Examples include:

  - Retail merchandise organized by type, such as women's clothing, men's clothing, luggage, and footwear.

  - Categories based on concepts. Try not to use numbers to distinguish among conceptual categories, since numbers imply a particular order. (On the other hand, colors might work well to reinforce categories when you don't want to suggest rank.)

support, and a conclusion; or using **categorical order.** See the accompanying feature for possible ways to organize your categories.

Make each screen as complete and independent as you can, while providing links to any related information that users might want or need. Remember that you can't count on users' reading your pages in any particular order, so each screen must make a reasonable amount of sense on its own. Sometimes it helps to write your screens in random order, so that you experience each chunk as a separate entity, the way users might.

Your goal, of course, is to make your text easy to read in the Web environment, with a visual structure that supports its message. You also want to take appropriate advantage of the dynamic, interactive capabilities of the Web. The next two sections talk about strategies for structuring your text for the Web. Subsequent sections talk about keeping your text ethical and persuasive.

Structuring Content Visually

Your primary goal, as you design your text, is to help users get the information they most need and that the site owners most want them to have. That means you must design your text so that the visual relationship of your content items reflects the logical relationship among those items. In other words, you need to create a clear visual hierarchy, using the relative size of elements on the page, their placement or position on the page, and their visual emphasis (see Figure 5.1). Larger items are perceived as more important. If you are designing in English, which is read from left to right and from top to bottom, items at the top left are likely to be noticed first. Visual emphasis created through color or bolding can draw users' attention, and color coding can guide users through related content. See the discussion of grouping in the preceding chapter for further suggestions on how to create a clear visual hierarchy.

Once your content has a clear visual hierarchy, then scanning it is much more likely to produce good comprehension and retention. The following guidelines, adapted from Jakob Nielsen (1997) and Crawford Kilian (1999), will also make your text easier to scan:

- Keep your text focused and concise.
- Start content chunks with summaries and clear main points.
- Use strong verbs and the active voice.
- Use lists.
- Use meaningful headings, subheadings, and summaries.
- Highlight key content information.

Figure 5.1   Dell's homepage uses the color, size, and position of headings and body text to organize its content. (See Figure 4.1 for a color version of this homepage.)

Keep Your Text Focused and Concise

A tight focus makes text easier to process. Typically, you'll want to stick to one main idea per paragraph. Make this focus clear in the first few words, to facilitate scanning. Remember, users will probably scan your content whether you want them to or not. If users skim the first few words and decide that this particular paragraph isn't relevant to their needs or goals, they probably won't read the rest. If that first sentence doesn't accurately reflect the rest of the paragraph's content, users may miss information that they need or that you want them to have.

Web text must also be very concise. For writers who are used to print documents, a good goal is to use half the words, or less, in writing Web text as compared to print text. Kilian (1999) suggests keeping paragraphs to about seventy-five words. Remember that online reading speeds are roughly 25 percent slower than print reading speeds, which means that you need to use fewer words (Nielsen, 1997). Also, reading long passages of text online causes eyestrain. Keep it short, or you're likely to lose readers.

You can often make text more concise by using headings and lists or by using phrases instead of sentences, as in Example 5.1. Your goal is to get your message across as efficiently as possible. Sometimes that means using more words, but usually, it means using fewer. Just remember to test your material with actual users; don't simply try to guess what will work best.

Example 5.1: Keeping Text Concise

Note that the revised version uses headings, lists, and phrases to keep the text short. It also avoids overt marketing hype.

Before

Travel Insurance Policies

We know that unexpected emergencies can happen to anyone, and we want your wonderful vacation to be worry-free. This cancellation and medical insurance can bring you peace of mind and protection in case you must cancel your trip because of a covered illness or some other covered emergency, or in case your trip is interrupted by a medical emergency.

This important coverage will provide for emergency medical evacuation, including airlift back to the United States, if necessary. It will cover necessary and reasonable medical expenses in the country where you are when the treatment becomes necessary. It will cover necessary and reasonable lodging costs for you and your travel companion during your medical care. It will cover reasonable travel expenses to return to the United States after your medical treatment is over. It will also cover 90 percent of your nonrefundable vacation expenses if your trip is interrupted.

Without this valuable coverage, you could end up spending thousands of dollars in emergency transportation, medical expenses, and housing as well as costs for hotel, airfare, or other trip cancellations. With our helpful coverage, you are also protected in the event of baggage loss or damage.

A covered illness includes any medical condition that would prevent your travel that is suffered by you, your traveling companion(s), or any immediate family member that did not begin or worsen during the sixty days prior to purchasing coverage.

Protect your vacation investment and get the peace of mind you deserve. Make the wise decision to apply for our travel insurance today. Simply fill out the application form and mail it in the enclosed postage-paid envelope today, and we'll do the rest. Your insurance coverage will be billed to your credit card, and you can relax, knowing that your vacation will be worry-free!

After

Travel Insurance Policy

What Is Covered

- Emergency medical evacuation
- Medical treatment during trip
- Lodging expenses for you and your travel companion(s) related to a medical emergency
- Travel expenses for you and your travel companion(s) related to a medical emergency
- 90 percent of nonrefundable vacation expenses if you must cancel your trip for medical reasons affecting you, your travel companion(s), or an immediate family member

What Is Not Covered

- Trip cancellation for medical conditions that began or worsened during the sixty days prior to purchasing insurance
- Trip cancellation for a reason other than a medical emergency that affects you, your travel companion(s), or an immediate family member

How to Apply

- Fill out the application form.
- Mail it in the enclosed postage-paid envelope.

You should also plan your screen layout to keep lines of text fairly short. Columns of online text should rarely, if ever, be wider than 4 to 5 inches, and even narrower columns of text may work well, depending on your layout. Unfortunately, the landscape layout of the computer screen, along with the smaller margins allowed by the screen, as opposed to paper, can lead unwary or inexperienced Web designers into long lines of text that are uncomfortable to read online.

Start Content Chunks with Clear Main Points

Put the conclusions and summaries first. Let the details follow. If there are lots of details that not all users will want, take advantage of the Web's link capabilities to put some of the information on another page.

Summaries should give as much information as possible, as concisely as possible. It can help to write the summary last, to make sure that it reflects the content accurately and completely. Avoid the tendency to build up to your conclusion. This pattern is natural, especially for students or beginners, but it can be deadly in a professional setting if users don't wait around for your stunning finish.

Writing a one-sentence summary for your entire site and one for each page will

- Help users decide whether or not to visit your site from a search engine list.
- Help other sites create appropriate links to your site, because they can use your summary to describe your site's content.
- Help orient users to your site when they arrive.

Use Strong Verbs and the Active Voice

Using strong verbs and the active voice will usually help keep your text short and to the point, and as we've already discussed, when it comes to Web text, shorter is almost always better than longer. Second, strong verbs and the active voice will keep your writing more energetic and natural, as in Example 5.2. The Web is probably the last place you can afford to sound pompous and artificially wordy.

If you are writing instructions, use simple command verbs and avoid long or complicated sentences.

Use Lists

Use bulleted or numbered lists, as appropriate. Lists are easier to scan than paragraphs, so users are much more likely to read and remember the information. Keep list items fairly short and make sure you organize the lists well. In other words, keep related list items together and make the relationship clear. Lists should never be a grab bag of unrelated items.

Example 5.2: Using Strong Verbs and the Active Voice

Before	After
Reformatting your data according to the template below is strongly encouraged. This reformatting will facilitate the processing of your survey results.	Use this optional template to reformat your survey results for faster processing.
Before	After
This insurance protection is provided in consideration of the payment in advance of the total required plan cost and will not cover losses suffered prior to purchase.	Your insurance will not cover losses that occur before you have paid in full.
Before	After
No insurance claim can be made after ninety days have elapsed between the time of the alleged incident and the time of claim submission.	After a loss occurs, you have only ninety days to file your insurance claim.

You should also try to keep list items grammatically parallel, which means that each item in a particular list should have the same grammatical structure, as demonstrated in Example 5.3. If one list item starts with a verb, all items in that list should start with a verb. If one list item is a complete sentence, all items in that list should be complete sentences. Parallel structure helps readers remember connected or similar items even if they don't consciously notice the parallelism. Thus, keeping list items grammatically parallel makes it easier for users to process your information.

Use Meaningful Headings and Subheadings

Users need to be able to predict the contents of the paragraph based on the heading, or they won't know whether or not to read the text in that section. Don't assume that users will read something just because you wrote it. Instead, help users recognize that your information will be valuable to them—by creating headings that are informative and that relate your content to users' goals and needs. Remember that your goal is *not* to see how much of your text you can get users to read; rather, your goal is to help users get all the information they need as quickly and enjoyably as possible.

Example 5.3: Using Parallel Structure

Not Parallel	Parallel
Your password must	Your password must
• Be six to eight characters in length.	• Be six to eight characters in length.
• Both letters and numbers must be included.	• Include both letters and numbers.
• Do not include words that can be found in the dictionary.	• Avoid words contained in a dictionary.

Not Parallel	Parallel
Refund policy:	Refund policy:
• We will accept most products returned within thirty days and refund your purchase price.	• You can return most undamaged items for a full refund for thirty days.
• Only unopened CDs and computer software.	• You can return unopened CDs and computer software for thirty days.
• No large items (over 27 inches in height or width) without prior authorization.	• You must obtain prior authorization before attempting to return large items (more than 27 inches in height or width).

Make sure titles and headings make sense when they appear out of context, as in Example 5.4. It's not only possible but probable that some of your page titles and headings will appear out of context, either in a list generated by a search engine or as a link on someone else's site. Remember, too, that users can access your site at nearly any point, so the page titles and headings need to orient users to where they are.

Make the first word in the heading a meaningful one; if all the headings start with the same word, users will have a harder time scanning the text quickly. And leave out articles like *the* or *a* in page titles; in an alphabetized list generated by a search engine, you'd hate to have your page show up under *the*.

Finally, keep headings grammatically parallel, for the same reasons that list items should be grammatically parallel.

Highlight Key Information

You can highlight key words and phrases using techniques for creating emphasis drawn from traditional document design, such as bolding, typeface, size, or

Example 5.4: Headings Should Make Sense out of Context

Notice that the revised headings below provide a clearer sense of the functionality they introduce.

Before	After
Enrollment	Enroll for Classes Online

Before	After
Schedule	Choose Your Spring Classes

Before	After
Introduction	How to Use Our Online Library

Before	After
Using the Personalized Prescription Tool	Find and Update Your Prescription Information

color. You can also highlight words by making them into links. Again, if possible, the highlighted words and phrases should be fairly self-explanatory, so that scanning the headings and the emphasized text leaves users with a sense of your overall message, as in Figure 5.2.

Highlighting a word affects users' reading speed. A bolded word can draw the users' eyes forward, encouraging them to skip over intervening text if they're in a hurry. But users' eyes will linger on the bolded word, slowing down their reading. Obviously, if you overuse bolding, you'll actually impede reading and comprehension. Use highlighting to make the overall message of the text easier to grasp at a glance. A useful guideline is to use headings and subheadings to make major points and highlighting to identify the primary support for those main points. Thus, users could grasp your overall message just by looking at the headings and subheadings and the highlighted text. To evaluate your success, try creating a wireframe with just the headings and subheadings and the highlighted text and see whether it makes sense.

Making the Most of Your Online Environment

The most important thing to remember about this new dynamic environment is that you are designing for screens, not pages. In your design, take advantage of online features:

- Add links to further information.
- Use scrolling appropriately.

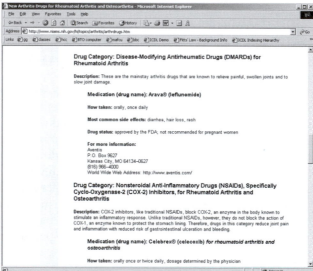

FIGURE 5.2   The text on these pages is easy to scan because each chunk of content is focused on one main idea, and the key words of each main idea are highlighted using blank space, bolding, bulleted lists, or color.

- Use frames cautiously, when appropriate.
- Include informational images and graphics.
- Use multimedia appropriately.
- Use interactivity appropriately.

Add Links to Further Information

Online, you can use linked pages to add more detail, allowing users to control the depth of the information they receive. In essence, you can let users shape their own path through the text, reading only the topics that interest them. Following a reference to a page that is not consecutive (either just before or just after the page you're on) is awkward and inconvenient in a print document but very easy with a link. Thus, computer documents can offer a lot more flexibility than print documents, and the cost of providing additional information can be pretty small—as long as you keep that information logically and conveniently accessible rather than letting it become confusing or overwhelming. Links are a powerful and handy tool that you can employ to design information to meet user needs.

Strategies for Using Links Effectively

An effective Web designer knows that it's what you call the link that makes it useful or not useful to your audience. Users should be able to predict what content they'll find by following a link based on the link text and its accompanying summary or description (see Example 5.5). Following links is time-consuming. If users follow a link that turns out not to be useful, they won't be eager to try your other links, and your credibility will suffer. It's your site—so it's your responsibility to make it easy for users to find all the information they want and need while bypassing insofar as possible the information that is not relevant for their purposes.

Some links are designed as graphics rather than text. If you use graphic links, remember to include a link description, along with the URL to which the link points, in the **ALT tag** for that image, so that visually impaired readers can still use the link. (The ALT tag allows you to associate a line of text with an image. Sighted users will see the text when they mouseover the image. Screen readers—software that reads screen content aloud—will read ALT text; otherwise screen readers simply indicate the presence of an image on the page while providing no clue as to what the image portrays.)

You may also want to cluster links to your sources or to other sites at the end of your material, so that you're not encouraging users to jump away to another site before they've seen what you have to say.

In some situations, it can seem helpful to have your external links open a new browser window, so that users can continue to browse your page while they wait for the new page to load. However, less experienced Web users are often confused by this strategy; such users may try unsuccessfully to click the "back" button to return to your site. If you do need to open a new window, make

Example 5.5: Make Links Informative

Before	After
Next	Next: Using Similarity to Group Objects

Before	After
Previous	Previous: Using Continuity to Show Logical Pathways

Before	After

Further Information	See also:
	     Using Contrast to Structure Information
	     Creating Visual Balance and Harmony

sure that the new window is smaller than the original window and has a clearly recognizable button for closing the window, so that users understand they are to read the extra content if they wish and then close the window. We recommend using **JavaScript,** a simple programming language that allows you to design interactive features on a website, to design a secondary window that has fewer buttons and requires less screen real estate.

Remember that the flexibility of links also means that users can arrive at your site virtually anywhere, so you must use your page design and your text—especially headings and page titles—to orient users to your material no matter where they begin.

Use Scrolling Appropriately

The fact that webpages can be scrolled provides both opportunities and challenges. Because not all users will scroll down, you must make sure that essential information appears above the scroll line—or *above the fold,* to use the term Web designers have borrowed from newspaper design. Start with your main points and use clear titles and summaries, or even a list of topics covered on the page, to make sure that users get the gist of the page without needing to scroll down. You can also use sidebars to present some of this overview information.

For example, Kathryn helped test a website that sells upscale cosmetics. This site's product pages had been designed with plenty of white space between the products shown on each page. Unfortunately, her early usability testing revealed that some users didn't realize they could scroll down to see more products. The site owners had to redesign the pages to provide a stronger visual clue to the full range of products available on each page.

Scrolling can provide tremendous design flexibility. Scrolling means you are no longer limited to exact page lengths. You are more free to group your content logically, then allow each content grouping to have its own page, despite variations in length. Of course, you have to group your content in ways that make sense. You don't want fifteen really short pages and one page that requires users to scroll endlessly!

Unfortunately, where the scroll line falls on your page will change depending on the setting of users' monitors. Some older monitors display 800 × 600 pixels, others display 1,024 × 728 pixels, and newer monitors can usually display 1,280 × 1,024 pixels or more. But some users choose to set their monitors to display 800 × 600 pixels in order to make the screen easier to read. Since you cannot control these settings, your best bet is to test your own pages during the design phase using different platforms and browsers, and with a variety of common monitor settings. This checking may seem time-consuming, but it will make your pages much friendlier for your users.

Use Frames Cautiously, When Appropriate

Using frames allows you to create scrolling and nonscrolling areas on the screen. Frames divide the browser window into sections, each of which contains a separate HTML document but which are displayed as if they were all part of the same page.

You can take advantage of scrolling and nonscrolling window areas to put summaries and crucial navigation information in nonscrolling areas while putting details into scrolling areas. Information or functions that users might need anywhere in the page should ideally be available at all times, which can be accomplished by putting them in a nonscrolling area. Be sure, however, that you make efficient use of the space above the scroll line or of nonscrolling areas. Don't waste that space on large logos, banner ads, or navigation options that users don't really want or need.

Creating a scrolling area on your page can also allow you to fit content into a section of the screen without having to shrink the text size, which would reduce readability.

Unfortunately, frames are an awkward technical solution to a real information need. Some kinds of documents are significantly easier to browse online if the table of contents remains constantly visible on the left margin. For example, online manuals or online reference materials are markedly easier to use if the table of contents stays visible. Unfortunately, frames have some serious usability problems. Inexperienced users often find it difficult to bookmark or print the pages that they want. Visually impaired users may not be able to find the content they need. Frames can also increase load times for the page and can be a problem for older browsers. Many experienced Web designers avoid frames because of these problems.

Include Informational Images and Graphics

Graphs, drawings, tables, and photographs are powerful tools for helping readers understand numbers and concepts quickly and accurately. Graphics and images can be easier and less expensive to incorporate and display online than in print—although they do have the cost of making pages load more slowly. Moreover, as you design a graphic for online display, you must plan for the lower resolution of screen display versus paper printing. Images that are fuzzy or overly reduced will not be very helpful to users.

Use graphics to

- Provide visual emphasis and draw attention to key information.
- Help users identify the things they see as they try to do a task.
- Help users visualize data, relationships, processes, and concepts.
- Help users see trends, summarize information, or make comparisons.
- Help users to remember information more vividly.
- Add visual drama to your site, contributing to the tone and feel you are trying to create.
- Provide a context for your data and communicate a message about it—establish a narrative.

Make sure you integrate text and graphics effectively, especially if the graphic is meant to help communicate your message. Keep the graphic as simple as possible and add any verbal explanations that users might need. Label the graphic clearly. Follow principles of good information design by choosing the kind of graphic that is most effective for your particular message and by locating the graphic as close as possible to the point that it explains. If necessary, include a thumbnail of complex images such as photographs for users who are reading quickly, allowing users who need or want to examine the image more closely to link to a larger version accompanied by additional text explanation.

Make sure you have ALT tags with explanatory text for users who deliberately browse with their graphics capability turned off or who are visually impaired. Never rely exclusively on graphics to convey crucial information. (See accompanying feature for additional tips on making your content accessible.)

Finally, if you borrow a graphic from another source, make sure you acknowledge the source and obtain proper permission.

Use Multimedia Appropriately

Research into how humans learn has shown that we typically learn better through a combination of words and images (Mayer, 2000) than we do from text alone. Dynamic images that can show change over time, or that allow users to interact with the content, can be even more powerful. The Web makes it fairly easy to combine words and images and even sound to create multimedia.

The evolution of multimedia content on the Web has followed a pattern:

Making Your Content Accessible

- Use the HTML "alt" tag to provide a simple text description of all graphics, images, or icons. Keep these text descriptions brief and check to see if they make sense out of context. Also describe the function of each graphic, if appropriate. Summarize key content of graphs and charts using the "longdesc" attribute.
- Provide detailed text descriptions for visual content (for example, a chart or diagram) or auditory content.
- Provide text equivalents or at least detailed descriptions for multimedia content.
- Consider providing non-text equivalents of text for nonreaders or users who have difficulty reading.
- If you have image links, make sure you've included text alternatives.
- Make sure link text makes sense when read out of context. (Many screen readers allow users to tab through the links on a page, so that only the link text is read.)
- Make sure links are big enough for users with impaired sight or reduced mobility (such as older users).
- Avoid blinking or moving text. Such text is less usable for most users, but it can be especially hard for users with disabilities and is impossible for most screen readers.
- Use headings, lists, and consistent structure for page content. Use style sheets where possible.
- Use row and column headers even for tables used as formatting devices, to make table content more understandable when accessed through screen readers. Remember that screen readers will read tables line by line.
- Avoid frames. If you can't, provide a "noframes" alternative.
- Provide links to download any plug-ins that may be required to view your content. Provide alternatives for plug-ins that may not be supported by assistive technologies.

1. Premature or excessive implementation of new technology, such as animated GIFs, streaming media, or **Flash** animation
2. Backlash against the new technology
3. A somewhat happy medium

Anytime you are considering adding multimedia content to your site, ask yourself whether you're doing so because multimedia is novel and exciting or whether, as you thought about your communications strategy, you came to the conclusion that it was the best way to achieve your communication goals. Resist the temptation to include gratuitous Flash introductory pages or multimedia just because you can. There are situations in which a multimedia approach is the best way to communicate with your audience and create meaning. For example, animation can be a good way to show transitions, to show change over time, or to help users visualize in three dimensions. Nationalgeographic.com uses Macromedia Flash to provide a multimedia history of Pearl Harbor (see Figure 5.3). It is an effective blend of music, images, and animation that is far more powerful than a static page with text and pictures could ever be.

When creating multimedia content, it can be tempting to include extra words, pictures, or sounds with the goal of maintaining user interest. However, keeping images and text carefully focused, making sure related images and text appear close together in space and time, and allowing users to control the pace of the presentation will make it easier for users to understand and remember your message.

Creating multimedia content can be expensive, so make sure you plan your multimedia content carefully before you move into production. Most content developers use storyboards, a technique developed by the film industry, to plan what content will appear on each major screen of the multimedia segment, and to plan what user actions and system responses are possible for that content. Your storyboard can be as simple as a piece of paper with a rough sketch of the screen and a brief list of user options and system responses.

Obviously, using multimedia implies certain tradeoffs in terms of download time, browser compatibility, and the fact that users must install the Flash plug-in or already have it installed. All of those issues have to be weighed when making the decision to use multimedia content. If you spend some time at http://www.whatsasthma.org/, you may conclude as we did that the use of Flash is very effective in providing a powerful education about how asthma works and how it can be treated (see Figure 5.4).

When offering multimedia, it is essential to give users the option of viewing your Flash interaction, or of viewing streaming video or audio media, but not require them to do so. Well-executed sites tend to offer two versions of their multimedia content—one straight HTML version that requires no plug-in and may require less bandwidth, and the complete version. We like this approach in most cases. It obviously makes sense to offer access to multimedia content in context. Some news sites include video or audio versions of news stories directly

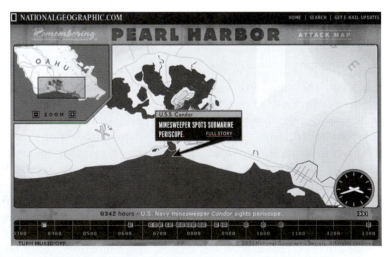

FIGURE 5.3   National Geographic's Multimedia History of Pearl Harbor

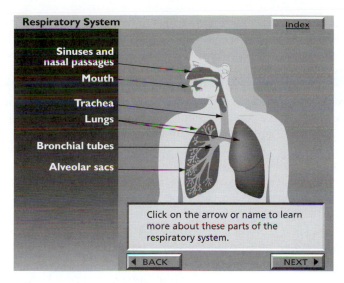

FIGURE 5.4   Using Flash Animation to Teach About Asthma

below links to the main HTML text/photo versions. Others prefer to have a photo/video section where all multimedia content is offered in the same place.

The important thing for you to remember is that Web content takes many forms, and although text remains the most important by far, you should be open to considering small doses of multimedia where appropriate. Higher production costs and longer project timelines are important to consider before beginning multimedia projects. But the end result can be far better.

Use Interactivity Appropriately

Perhaps one of the most revolutionary aspects of Web text, as opposed to print text, is the opportunity it presents for interactivity. As discussed above, users can shape their own reading experience through the links they select. The Web also provides the opportunity for users to request content that is shaped to their particular needs. For example, landsend.com allows users to see clothing displayed on a model that reflects their own body measurements. Cascadia.net, a business-system consulting firm, uses Flash to provide real-time estimates of implementation times and costs for users who want to configure an online store (http://www.cascadia.net/StoreBuilder/). Some sites generate their webpages dynamically, responding to user requests for particular content.

Interactivity can also be a persuasive tool. Sometimes your website is primarily about providing information—for example, if you're creating an educational site or a support or an intranet site. But often clients want to persuade consumers to use a particular service, or they want to develop some kind of ongoing relationship with them. Even if you're mostly providing information, you may want to persuade your users that that information meets their needs. Or you may want to persuade users to adopt a particular point of view. Interactivity can help you by involving your users in your message and by making it easier for users to act when they have been persuaded.

Both con artists and effective salespeople also know that if your persuasive goal is to get users to act in some way—to make a purchase, use a service, join an organization, or fill out a survey—then you can encourage that action by building a pattern of active agreement and involvement. The difference between con artists and salespeople lies in how ethical their communication is. We discuss the ethical decisions involved in establishing your credibility with users and keeping your content ethical in subsequent sections.

Think about the actions you (or your clients) want users to take as well as what actions the users themselves might want to take. Then make those actions as easy and available as possible: let users purchase whatever you're selling or make reservations or join in the conversation or get further information or send e-mail to someone who can act on their behalf. Make it easy for users to act in the way you wish and provide an incentive, as appropriate, for users to act quickly.

Furthermore, as you write the text for your website, pay attention to how your words call users to action. You can make users feel empowered by asking for their vote or their participation in some common cause, increasing the likelihood that they will continue to act in other ways. Show users that a particular action will solve a problem that they care about. If appropriate, you can give examples of good results that come from taking action or of bad results that come from failing to act.

Remember, however, that the Web doesn't really work well as an intrusive communication medium. Too often, Web content is seen in terms of advertising—a deliberate attempt to break into user awareness in order to convey a client-driven message. That model simply doesn't work for websites, which is why banner ads are mostly ineffective. Users are on your site because they chose to come, and you'd better figure out why they came and help them meet those goals, or they won't stay.

Make Content Easy to Find

Let's face it. The main reason we all love the Web is because we can find stuff there. Lots of Web experiences today begin by getting up close and personal with a search engine. Clearly, your website and its content need to be easy to find. And the key to that is good **metadata,** or data about your data. In other words, your site needs to begin with a clear summary description and a carefully chosen set of keywords that will help search engines find your site and its content effectively. Include likely synonyms for your keywords as well, so that a search for "cheddar" on your site about "adventures in cooking" will still take visitors to the page about how to make homemade cheese. And, since not everyone spells perfectly, you may want to include a few common misspellings for particularly important keywords.

Information architects talk about three kinds of metadata:

- Descriptive—information about what the content item is (a photo of my dog)
- Intrinsic—information about what the content item is made of, or how it was made (a 36KB JPEG)
- Administrative—information about how the content item should be handled or who made it or where it came from (photographer John, created 5/16/2003, published 8/18/2003)

Metadata not only makes your site content easier to find, it also makes your site easier to update or revise. Good metadata about your content can help later developers make their subsequent additions to the site stylistically and thematically consistent.

Establishing Credibility

Ultimately, to be persuasive, you must convince users that you (or your client) know what you're talking about and that you mean them well. You have to gain credibility. Unless you first establish your credibility, you have no hope of persuading users to act.

The most powerful way to gain credibility and to persuade users that you mean them well is to focus on their needs. If you are helping users achieve their goals and making the experience reasonably enjoyable, users are likely to return to your site and recommend it to others.

You also gain credibility through professional-looking design and high-quality writing. You can increase your credibility by

- *Being clear about who created the site and about what the site's goals are.* Users want to be able to evaluate your knowledge and expertise as well as your motivations. (Crawford Kilian [1999] points out that surprising readers with new information with which they are likely to agree can dramatically enhance your credibility, making you sound like an expert with opinions similar to those users already have.)
- *Avoiding manipulation, excessive hype, or bias.* Promotional language not only affects users' perception of your motives but can also make your site harder to use. (See the accompanying feature about Nielsen's experiments in website usability.)
- *Staying focused on users rather than the company.* Too often, company websites frustrate users by focusing on how great the company is rather than on what users might want or need. As Kilian points out, company representatives are often more focused on users in person than they

remember to be on the Web: the sales rep works hard to make sure you can find the car you need, and the successful loan officer is much more focused on identifying the specific financial products you need than on rattling off a nonstop list of everything the bank has available. But clients can lose track of the interactive nature of their service when they think about creating a website—perhaps because they can't see the users. Participatory design and usability testing can help forestall this problem (see Chapters 3 and 6).

> ### Jakob Nielsen: Effective Writing for the Web
>
> Nielsen compared online text in various forms, to see which text characteristics were easier for readers to process. As we discussed earlier in this chapter, he found that reading speeds and retention rates went up for text that was brief, used headings and lists, highlighted key words, and presented summaries followed by expanded details.
>
> Nielsen also found that reading speeds and retention rates increased for text that used nonpromotional language. He suggests that promotional language may have decreased user reading speed and retention because, although today's readers are experienced at reading past hype, doing so imposes an additional cognitive burden.

- *Sounding friendly, direct, and relatively informal.* Even conservative sites such as the *Wall Street Journal* tend to sound more direct and less formal on the Web than they do in print. But you must be careful to adopt the level of formality or informality that is appropriate for your particular client, the client's business, and users' expectations of the site. The tone of The Motley Fool site will be much more informal and lighthearted than that of the *Wall Street Journal* site.

- *Including links to other sites.* Good links show that you've done your research and reinforce the impression that you have users' interests at heart.

In this skeptical age, you probably won't get very far by claiming that you have only the users' interests at heart or that you're aiming to satisfy their needs at the expense of your own. Most savvy users expect you to be well intentioned but not stupid. You'll be more persuasive, and ultimately more successful, if you can show that what you offer or advocate is mutually beneficial. Obviously, most of your effort should go into details, facts, and figures that demonstrate how users can benefit from your suggestions. It can also help to address common user concerns or possible objections, perhaps through a frequently asked questions page. If you sound fair about objections or drawbacks, users are more likely to trust your conclusions.

Keeping Your Communication Ethical

Whenever you are providing information or services to others, your actions can have important consequences for their welfare. Although it may be tempting to focus exclusively on information that supports the user beliefs or behaviors you wish to promote, while glossing over or even omitting information that might cause users to act in ways you don't want, doing so has important legal and moral consequences. It may seem advantageous to exaggerate your—or your client's—abilities or the quality of offered products, but such exaggeration may be both dishonest and harmful to others. You are responsible for the work that you do: you can't just say you did what the client or your boss wanted.

Some ethical dilemmas are more obvious than others. It is clearly unethical to lead others to make a choice or perform an action that is not to their best advantage by giving them inaccurate or incomplete or deliberately misleading information. It is clearly unethical to harm others deliberately or through negligence, especially in pursuit of your own interests. It is also unethical to make promises you don't intend to keep in your effort to persuade others. Such ethical violations frequently carry legal penalties. For example, the tobacco industry has been penalized for deliberately and/or carelessly misleading consumers about the physiological effects of nicotine. Other ethical situations may be more complicated and will require careful decision making on your part.

Ethical communication depends on your honesty, fairness, and concern for others. We all have a responsibility to make thoughtful ethical decisions and not let others make our ethical decisions for us. You need to think carefully about your obligations to yourself as a person of integrity, to your team, to your client, to your users, and to the community at large. If these obligations conflict, make good choices—choices that contribute to the welfare of the greatest number of people. You should probably consider the following questions:

- What principles do I care about in this situation?
- What are my obligations to others (including users, coworkers, employers, and the community)?
- What are the probable consequences of my actions, for myself and others?

You will inevitably face pressure at some point to engage in unethical communication. Common pressures include the desire to increase profits or market share or a demand that you stay "loyal" to the team or to the company. Don't let others make your ethical decisions for you or pressure you into doing something you will later regret.

Unethical behavior does have legal consequences as well as moral ones. Even if your unethical behavior doesn't land you or your client in jail, a reputation for integrity and good service is crucial to the long-term growth of a business. A degree of trust and honesty is also necessary for society to keep functioning. Technical communicators, like other professionals, have a responsibility to meet professional standards of good communication practice.

The most serious unethical behaviors in website design include manipulating your data, using deliberately misleading or ambiguous language, exaggerating claims, or concealing information that your users need in order to make good decisions.

Unethical behavior in website design also includes plagiarism, or stealing proprietary information. Even if someone gives you permission to borrow their code, you need to provide acknowledgment. You cannot legally use someone else's graphics or text without permission. (See the website accompanying this textbook for further discussion of copyright issues.)

Editing Your Content

Editors may focus on ensuring that a document meets company policy or complies with a company style guide, on making sure that all sections match one another, on proofreading for errors or mechanics, or on verifying that all text is clear and that all graphics are correct and fully integrated with the text.

However, editing includes a lot more than eliminating grammatical errors or making a document conform to a particular style guide. Certainly, these problems should be taken care of in the editing stage, but the true focus of editing, as with every other writing or Web design activity, is meeting user needs. Editors should be thinking about users as they make decisions about language, sentence structure, tone, and visual focus. A good editor works on the final coordination of every element of the document—the language, the integration between text and graphics, the document design, as well as the stylistic consistency. Editors can help keep the level of detail or the conceptual structure consistent throughout the site. For this reason, it's usually not effective to try to edit your own writing; you need a fresh set of eyes and an unbiased perspective, which is hard to come by when you're looking over your own masterpiece right after months of labor.

To make editing more productive, consider proofreading with a partner, pacing your editing sessions, and using editing checklists, to stay focused on key elements as you go through the document. Proofread both on screen and using printouts. Follow an agreed-upon style guide or style sheet, to reduce conflict on less crucial elements and promote consistency. A style guide helps you decide what will be considered "correct" when a choice between alternatives must be made.

See the website accompanying this text for some exercises on editing for conceptual and stylistic consistency. You should also review your site carefully using the checklist below.

Testing Your Content for Effectiveness

The most important tool you have for ensuring that your content is effective is usability testing. Testing can help you determine whether your design and writing choices make sense to users, whether you've provided the information that users need to accomplish their goals and tasks, and whether it is structured in a way that is comprehensible to users and easy for them to use. Usability testing is also the best way to make sure that your content will work effectively for international users, if they are part of your target audience. The next chapter walks you through the process of performing usability testing on your site.

✔ **FINAL CHECKLIST**

User Focus

- Does your content focus on what users need or want? Do you show readers why content might be important to them, in terms of their goals and priorities?
- Is content arranged to meet users' needs and priorities?

Scannability

- Is the text brief and focused?
- Are your text columns narrow enough to facilitate reading (but not too narrow)?
- Have you used headings and subheadings effectively? Do the headings allow users to accurately predict the content that they introduce?
- Does your link text allow users to accurately predict the content behind each link?
- Do headings and link text employ the users' language and labels?
- Have you used lists, where appropriate, to make the text easier to scan?

Tone

- Do you avoid excessive formality in tone? Is the tone appropriately friendly?
- Do your content and layout support the relationship you want to build with users?
- If your site is likely to reach an international audience, have you avoided culture-specific idioms? Have you used color appropriately?
- If you have included humor, is it appropriate and inoffensive? If you are likely to have readers from other cultures, will it make sense to those readers?

Information Design

- Is all the information necessary to perform each task available when and where it is required?
- Have you provided multiple paths to important information, as necessary?
- Is your format consistent from page to page? Are headings and other key text formatted consistently?
- If you have included multimedia, does it support your communication goals?

- Do your pages make sense out of context, in case users arrive somewhere in the middle of your site?
- If your pages require scrolling, have you made sure that the most essential information appears above the fold?

Images and Graphics

- Do your images contribute to the site's success? Is their contribution great enough to justify the added download time?
- Are your informational graphics successfully integrated with your text? Is each graphic well labeled? Did you include good explanatory text using the ALT tag?
- Have you used color appropriately to support your communication goals? Does it make your content easier to access and easier to understand?

Ethical Considerations

- Have you kept your content ethical, by avoiding exaggerated claims or misleading information?
- Have you provided clear information about who created the site and about the site's purpose?
- Have you included information about when the site was last updated, to help users evaluate the quality of the content you provide?
- Have you included links to other sites, if appropriate?
- If you borrowed graphics from another source, have you obtained proper permissions and provided proper acknowledgment?

Quality Control

- Have you eliminated spelling, punctuation, and syntax errors?
- Have your graphics reproduced well?
- Do your pages display effectively in different browsers and on different platforms?
- Have you made it easy for users to send you feedback about your site?

REFERENCES

Kilian, Crawford. 1999. *Writing for the Web.* Vancouver: Self-Counsel Press.
Locker, Kitty. 1999. *Business and Administrative Communication.* 5th ed. New York: Irwin.
Mayer, Richard. 2001. *Multimedia Learning.* New York: Cambridge University Press.

Nielsen, Jakob. 1997. "Concise, Scannable, and Objective: How to Write for the Web."
http://www.useit.com/alertbox/9710a.html.

Price, Jonathan, and Lisa Price. 2002. *Hot Text: Web Writing That Works.* Indianapolis:
New Riders.

Reeves, Byron, and Clifford Nass. 1996. *The Media Equation: How People Treat Computers, Television, and New Media Like Real People and Places.* Cambridge, U.K.:
Cambridge University Press.

Schriver, Karen. 1997. *Dynamics in Document Design: Creating Texts for Readers.* New
York: Wiley.

6 Usability Analysis

CHAPTER HIGHLIGHTS

What Is a Usability Test?
   Definition of Usability
   Using Simplified Usability Test Methods
The Usability-Testing Process
   Developing the Test Plan
   Selecting and Recruiting Test Participants
   Preparing the Test Materials and Setting Up the Testing Environment
   Conducting the Test
   Transforming Data into Findings and Recommendations
Presenting Results
   Video Summary of Findings
   Ethical Video Editing

As we have seen throughout this book, effective website design is user-centered, not technology- or function-centered. In Chapters 2–5, we described how to go into the field and develop insight about users as well as how to leverage this user insight to make decisions about your website's navigation, information architecture, visual design, and content. By this point in the design process, you have created:

- Personas
- Task flows
- Site maps
- Wireframes
- Visual designs
- Textual and other content

All of your activities have resulted in a **prototype** of your new site. So is it time to launch? Not yet. Even if you are an experienced interaction designer, your prototype still represents only a *first draft*—your earliest attempt at responding to what you've learned about user behaviors with an interaction design. You now need to conduct a series of iterative **usability** tests—revising your prototype based on what you learn.

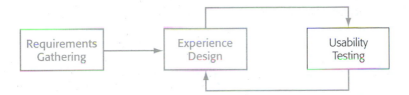

What Is a Usability Test?

We want to be clear about what we mean by *usability test.* As Jeffrey Rubin (1994) points out, the term is sometimes used rather indiscriminately to describe *any* technique for evaluating a website. When we use the term *usability testing,* we're referring to a method that involves representatives of the website's target population conducting tasks so we can evaluate how well a website meets specific usability criteria. Real people, doing real tasks. Not people *talking* about what they do. And definitely not people talking about what they *might* do in the future.

Definition of Usability

ISO 9241, the definition of usability established by the International Organization for Standardization (known as ISO) is well known. Although some important leaders in the field modify this definition occasionally, it is a good place to start.

According to the ISO, the usability of an interface is a measure of the effectiveness, efficiency, and satisfaction with which specified users can achieve specified goals in a particular environment with that interface.

- *Effectiveness = the accuracy and completeness with which specified users can achieve specified goals.* In other words, can users do what you want them to be able to do on your site—find an 800 number, buy a book, schedule a class, and so forth?

  Metric: success rate. When we're attempting to measure the "effectiveness" part of our definition of usability, we sometimes measure success rate or error rate. If we were testing a library website and our scenario were "Find out how many overdue library books you have," we'd note how many participants got the right answer. Error rate is significant because even if all test participants are eventually able to find the answer, when a majority of the participants commit frequent and/or similar errors, we know that the interface makes the task too difficult.

- *Efficiency = the resources expended in relation to the accuracy and completeness of goals achieved.* In other words, how much pain did users have to endure before they could successfully complete tasks?

Metric: time on task. When we want to measure the "efficiency" part of our definition of usability, we sometimes use a stopwatch to measure how long it takes participants to complete tasks. Time-on-task numbers can be compared with other versions of the same interface or even with competitors' websites that support the same tasks.

- *Satisfaction = the comfort and acceptability of the work system to its users and other people affected by its use.* In other words, did people like it?

Metric: subjective. Many usability professionals conduct debriefings at the end of their usability tests and ask users to provide feedback about the overall user experience or specific features of it.

Although we think ISO 9241 provides a useful definition, we want to make an important point. Usability involves a lot more than the ability to create numbers about success rate, how long it took users to check out, or their "satisfaction." The most important insights we gain from usability testing are qualitative, and they're hard to capture with numbers. Good usability testing is about how you interpret your data in order to fix problems and improve websites. There is a lot that happens during a usability test that gets missed even by experienced professionals who produce seemingly detailed reports.

We like how Jeffrey Rubin (1994, 19) describes it: "Any doctor can measure a patient's vital signs such as blood pressure and pulse rate. But interpreting those numbers and recommending the appropriate course of action for a specific patient is the true value of the physician." How much you learn from usability testing is likely to increase as your expertise, experience, and insight grow.

We don't want to discourage first-time usability testers by suggesting that you won't gain valuable insight, though. Quite the opposite. You don't need a Ph.D. in an experimental science to conduct an effective usability test and improve your website—and we'll show you how.

The specific approach we choose depends on our objectives as well as very practical considerations, such as how much time and money are available. But certain basic steps are common to all forms of usability testing, regardless of whether we're testing our very first paper prototype or doing a final benchmark test of a launched site. Namely, we

1. Recruit a small number of representative users (anywhere from six to twelve).
2. Invite them to perform tasks on the site.
3. Observe them and evaluate usability problems.
4. Report our findings.

Focus groups are not usability tests. Notice that as we described usability testing, we talked about representative users' actually conducting tasks on a website. Focus groups involve a small number of people discussing their preferences. Preference data is relevant, however, only after people have interacted with a design concept. And it reveals little about what people actually do.

"Heuristic" evaluations are not usability tests. Heuristics (or accepted usability principles from the body of research and human-factors literature) are simple;

PROFESSIONAL PROFILE *Jeffrey Rubin*

Doing Usability, or Zen "Beginner's Mind"

The Usability Group

One of Jeff Rubin's most valuable contributions to the field of usability research is the sheer clarity of his *Handbook of Usability Testing* (1994), a consistent bestseller in the field. Rubin has a knack for explaining usability in practical terms, in a way that connects with people's experience and makes usability seem like common sense. By taking the mystery out of usability, he has helped to make it easier for people to learn how to do effective usability research. At the same time, he has been dedicated to developing new methods of user research and usability testing, and his work is highly valued by usability professionals.

Rubin got into usability research by accident. He had originally planned to use his training in experimental psychology in a clinical or social-work setting. But Bell Labs in the 1970s was looking for psychologists to help the company develop usable mainframe telecommunications systems, and so he joined one of the very first industrial usability-testing labs. The Bell Labs team was focused on conducting solid, practical human-factors research that would be rapid, yet thorough and comprehensive. Rubin's commitment to practical research design, achievable in a business setting, was formed at Bell Labs and became the foundation for his career as a usability consultant and later his book on testing. Currently, as principal of The Usability Group, Jeff's main focus is the strategic role of customer experience and usability research in the development of technology initiatives.

Rubin feels that three primary skill sets are involved in creating effective websites: analysis skills, design skills, and evaluation skills. Webworkers need to have exposure to all three skill sets, but he feels it is natural to gravitate toward a particular stage of the process depending on one's interests.

According to Rubin, good analysis begins with establishing a clear business case for a site, tied to the needs and values of the intended audience. This is followed by qualitative and quantitative research on the targeted segments, work modeling, the development of customer profiles and task analyses within a business context, and the creation of customer-centered and -validated requirements for design. Not establishing this foundation is like building a house without a blueprint. Rubin feels so strongly about this analysis that he believes he can predict a site's success or failure simply based on a client's commitment to this phase and the rigor with which it is carried out.

continued on next page

Rubin compares designing software to filmmaking. Just as filmmakers create storyboards before any film is shot, Rubin insists that everything about your Web interaction should be on paper before you start production. He strongly recommends against bridging directly to interactive prototypes from the analysis, warning that designers are likely to end up prematurely committed to inappropriate design concepts and paths, even if they later test the prototypes with users. He recommends using paper prototypes to do work modeling and preliminary testing with users.

Rubin's advice to usability professionals comes out of the thirty years he has spent studying Buddhist philosophy. Since we all share the tendency to be overly influenced and conditioned by previous experience, we may short-circuit the problem-solving process by inappropriately reapplying a design or solution that worked for a past situation, or we may generalize across an entire audience. Instead, Rubin recommends that professionals approach every new project with what's known in the Zen tradition as "beginner's mind." "Beginner's mind" is an attitude and outlook that is both humble and aware of the uniqueness of the present situation. Focusing on a deep understanding of one's particular audience, its nuances and cultural idiosyncrasies, enables us to create products that work on the functional, economic, and artistic levels.

human behavior is complex. **Heuristic usability evaluations**—or expert reviews, as we prefer to call them—are a very useful preparatory exercise. However, busy project teams sometimes employ expert reviews as a way to get out of conducting a real usability test. Expert reviews should never replace observation of actual users doing actual tasks.

We also want to point out that an expert review is most helpful when the "expert" conducting the review has spent many hours observing and conducting real tests with real users and has no involvement with the project. Those who have merely studied theory are less likely to catch usability problems. In our experience, people—regardless of their education level—who have observed numerous usability studies with real users are more likely to spot usability problems.

We use expert reviews in the early stages of website development (during the creation of wireframes), when major usability problems abound. It is not necessary to bring in participants for a usability test to reveal the obvious, such as missing or inconsistent navigation bars, jargon or graphics that the target users won't understand, or lack of feedback from the site about what users should do next (see the accompanying feature on usability principles that should be considered in a heuristic evaluation). However, expert reviews by even the most experienced leaders in the field still miss serious usability issues that present major barriers to user success. Expert reviews can help you prepare for usability testing, but they are no substitute for usability testing.

Using Simplified Usability Test Methods

Fortunately, usability tests don't have to be fancy in order to provide valuable information. Usability testing traces its roots to classical methods for conducting a controlled experiment. In those more academic applications of research, a specific hypothesis is formulated and then tested by isolating variables under controlled conditions. Cause-and-effect relationships are examined with the appropriate inferential statistical techniques; then the hypothesis is either confirmed or rejected.

If you were going to try to apply true experimental research design to your usability testing, you would need a specific hypothesis, a very systematic method for randomly choosing participants who constitute an appropriate sample of your population, tight experimental controls so that each participant had identical experience prior to and during the test as well as identical interaction with the moderator, control groups varying only on the single variable you are testing, and a big enough sample that you could measure differences among groups statistically.

You simply will not have the time or the money to follow that kind of methodology. We wouldn't recommend it even if you did. It's just not appropriate, because usability testing isn't about formulating or testing classical hypotheses under controlled conditions or obtaining quantitative proof. The whole point of usability testing is to get qualitative information about how to fix problems and redesign websites—quickly.

Usability Principles That Experts Check Before Conducting Usability Tests

The following list is adapted from Jeffrey Rubin (www.usability.com).

- *Concept:* The site's conceptual framework matches the best guess regarding users' mental model and typical usage. The value proposition is clear and compelling.
- *Content:* Text and graphics match users' domain knowledge or background.
- *Consistency:* Page layout, labels (links, buttons), field formats, window and page titles, terminology, and the like are consistent both among windows within the site and with the conventions of the larger Web.
- *Feedback:* Visual or other feedback to user actions is provided within a reasonable time.
- *Navigation:* Users can find tasks and information, link labels are effective, the breadth versus depth is appropriate, and the "back" button is not the only means of returning to a page.
- *Terminology:* No technical or domain jargon is employed unless it's appropriate for users.
- *Visibility:* The visual display of information, chunking, grouping, sequencing, format, and alignment of text/graphics are clear, and icons are recognizable.
- *Recognition, not recall:* Users do not have to remember information from one part of a process to another.

PROFESSIONAL PROFILE *Jakob Nielsen*

Making Usability "Usable"

Principal, Nielsen-Norman Group

When Jakob Nielsen talks about growing up in Denmark, it makes sense that he went on to become one of the most important people in the field of usability. He had early exposure to psychological research through his father's work as a professor. And careful attention to people and behavior was further encouraged by his mother's clinical role as a psychologist specializing in children.

His first experience with computers came in high school, in 1973. That first "personal" computer (it was a single-user mainframe) took up an entire room and had 5 kilobytes of memory. He spent significant time experimenting with its possibilities, writing programs, and trying to make it do things.

However, when Jakob moved on to the university, his experience with newer, supposedly "better" computers was different. The new computers were time-shared, complicated, and did not provide any direct, real-time feedback or response. Although more powerful and faster, they were very hard to use—and he wondered whether he and his classmates were really getting more done, despite the added power. At the time, he was reading Ted Nelson's books about how computer information devices had the potential to be liberating for human beings, allowing them to reach out to one another in a worldwide hypertext system. The contrast between Nelson's ideas about the potential of computers and the day-to-day user experiences of Jakob and his fellow students was profound.

These three influences—behavioral study, computers that were painfully difficult to use, and the vision of computers as liberating—came together as a choice for an early thesis topic, and Jakob has never looked back from that initial drive to make computers usable. In fact, for many people, his name has become synonymous with usability.

Perhaps one of his biggest contributions to the field involved making usability research itself more widely "usable." Traditional usability testing grew out of the rigorous experimental methods of psychology and involved large controlled experiments that were complicated, costly, and necessarily rare. However, his research has shown that more applied usability methods—methods he calls "discount usability"—can still provide valuable usability information.

With seven or eight test participants and a more qualitative approach, "discount usability" is easier to fit into the product design cycle and is there-

continued on next page

fore more likely to occur. "Discount usability" became a paradigm shift that helped transform the entire field.

Jakob also helped to refocus the Web design world on the quality of the user experience with his emphasis on simplicity and usability in Web design. Jakob started making this argument in 1994, after his first few studies of Web and intranet usability. He found that users want information that's quickly accessible and focused, without bells or whistles. Now, with 500 million users in his corner on this issue, Jakob's tenets on simplicity in Web design have become widely accepted.

When asked what skills are most crucial for the success of usability professionals, Jakob talks about the importance of observational skills. Good usability professionals need to be careful observers and know how to take their observations and turn them into design principles and design ideas. Usability professionals must be able to see what's going on during a test and then figure out the story behind those specific observations—what's going on in terms of principles. Although his background and path to success show that he obviously values university training as a great starting place, Jakob also believes that observational skills and experience matter more than getting a particular degree. He insists, too, that there is no substitute for experience: usability professionals must have users try many designs for different tasks under many circumstances before they can reliably draw conclusions from what they see.

The Usability-Testing Process

The usability-testing process involves:

1. Developing the test plan
2. Selecting and recruiting test participants
3. Preparing the test materials and setting up the testing environment
4. Conducting the test
5. Transforming the data into findings and recommendations

Before we discuss the testing process, however, we'd like to point out that there are two variations to our method for usability testing. The first is designed to assess prototypes and is usually an **iterative usability test.** We do three or four iterative tests during the design process. The second is meant to measure or validate an existing or almost completed site. We usually call it a **benchmark usability test.** When we can, we do two benchmark tests, one before we begin the redesign (if there's an existing site) and one on our final product.

As we present the overall usability-testing process, we'll explain how you modify certain steps during iterative or benchmark testing. The differences between the two methods are not radical. During an iterative test, the moderator may interact with participants or have them "think aloud." You may not even capture success rates or use a stopwatch to measure time on task. Iterative tests tend to be more focused on a couple of major scenarios and on catching big obstacles that stop users from being successful. You don't care about measuring how bad the problem is; you just want to learn where the problem is so you can fix it.

During a benchmark test, however, you'll sometimes be more formal. Participants could sit in a test room while the moderator observes through a one-way mirror (if you have access to a fully equipped usability lab). You won't interrupt participants or converse with them during the test, and especially if you're trying to measure time on task, the participants won't "think aloud." You'll learn any subjective perceptions about the experience in a posttest interview.

Developing the Test Plan

Developing your test plan includes setting goals for your test and deciding what to test. You'll also make some preliminary decisions about which user groups you want to test, so that you can plan your test accordingly. Selecting and recruiting your test participants is discussed more thoroughly in the next subsection.

Your test goals are then captured in a test script—a collection of sample tasks that you ask users to perform. We begin by describing a test script and providing an example. We then discuss the two major types of test scripts—feature-focused test scripts and user-focused, or exploratory, test scripts—and how to decide which type to use. We finish by discussing how to check the effectiveness of your script in a pilot test.

Writing a Test Script

The moderator uses a **test script** to structure each session. The meat of the script is usually a table with two columns, as in Example 6.1. On the left is a series of about three to four tasks or questions the moderator assigns or asks participants, and on the right is space to record what users say and do. The tasks (sometimes called scenarios in the literature) and questions you assign will reflect a mix of business and user goals. For example, while working on a consumer medication site recently, Michael and his team spent several days in the company's call center, where they listened to customers asking dosage questions. An example question for one of their usability tests became, "Your neighbor knows you have Internet access. She's asked you to go to ProductName.com's website to find the right dosage for her baby. Her baby weighs 22 pounds. Let me watch what you would do."

As in the sample script shown in Example 6.1, we like to make the tasks in our test scripts as realistic as possible. The artificial environment of a usability test room is obviously not the best place to discover user goals. Instead, build on what you learned by observing users in context. Remember that after your field observations of users in Chapter 2, you made detailed task flows of how they worked and what mattered to them about their process. The tasks you write

Example 6.1: Usability Test Script

[NameReplaced].com Usability Test Plan
Test date: [to be determined]
Test location: Murray Hill Center, New York, N.Y.

What the Moderator Says and Does	What the Respondent Says and Does
1. Here is $50 that is yours to spend on this site any way you wish. Being sure to "think out loud" each step of the way, let me watch what you would do (abbreviated as LMWWYWD). Now that you've had a chance to do things the way you would do them on your own, I'm going to assign you some predefined tasks so I can see how easy/difficult specific things are to do:	
2. You've heard that BOBBI BROWN has some great lipstick shimmers, and you want to see them. LMWWYWD. [Follow-up: Which one is your favorite? Does that same color come in a blush? Can you find a blush to match your lipstick?]	
3. How much is a half-ounce bottle of COCO parfume [Chanel]?	
4. You want to get your boyfriend a gift—a men's shaving product from Clinique. LMWWYWD.	

4a. Let's pretend you decide to get the same thing for your father for Father's Day in June, so you want to remember this particular product. LMWWYWD (if you were at home). [Prompt: "Add to Favorites." What is this? What is the site asking you to do? Would you become a member? Why would you become a member?]	
4b. Let's pretend you've decided you want to become a member. LMWWYWD.	
5. Let's imagine that your sister had some beauty concern that she wanted advice about. Try to find a solution to her particular concern. LMWWYWD.	
(Your script would be much longer than this, since this is just an example.)	
[Conclusion]	
[Administer posttest.]	

into your test script should reflect what you've learned about user processes as well as the business goals of the site.

Because the average usability test lasts about an hour, and some sites are quite large, prioritizing what to test can sometimes be tough.

Feature-Focused Test Scripts

One approach to writing test scripts is client- and feature-focused. Designers who are already invested in an idea or a concept they've produced want to find out whether it works or whether it has appeal. They might say, "Find out whether the 'My Stocks' section works" or "Test the registration process." The advantage to this more moderator-driven approach is that it allows you to move test respondents quickly among relatively unrelated areas of the site and maximize the amount of feedback you get.

The disadvantage is that by directing users to a specific area on the screen, you might encourage them to spend more time figuring out the interface than they would under normal conditions. You have no guarantee that they would have noticed that feature or section at all if they were not sitting in a usability lab, with you prompting them about to where to go and what to focus on.

Because you've used all of the techniques described in Chapters 2–5, you have probably already met many representative users in the field, and you have already developed a feel for the kinds of tasks that they perform and what matters to them about their process. So even if you create a feature-focused script in which you assign all of the scenarios without allowing users to create any of their own, you can still be confident that those scenarios have value. Without a foundation in early user research, feature-focused scripts are less grounded in realistic user tasks and are more likely to leave major problems to be discovered by actual users later.

User-Focused/Exploratory Test Scripts

In a more user-focused test script, participants conduct scenarios—interacting only with the elements of the site that they notice and choose while trying to accomplish a goal. You might even allow them to set their own goals rather than assigning them specific tasks.

Whether you write all the tasks or allow users to create a few of their own, with user- and scenario-focused test scripts, it is possible for users to pass over aspects of the site about which you need feedback. Of course, if your goal is to test the registration process, a scenario that requires users to register is likely to get you what you're looking for—feedback about the usability of the registration process. However, there may be a piece of content that you want users to interact with that they completely ignore. When you do your first usability testing, you'll be surprised to discover all the assumptions you have made about how you think people will use your site.

Thus, an important drawback of the scenario-focused method is that as test participants attempt to perform a task or solve a problem, they may not even use the navigation scheme designers are anxious to evaluate. However, user-driven scenarios do allow you to learn how well the site meets some of its larger business goals—for example, customer retention or acquisition. A less moderator-prompted and -controlled test script can allow you to determine how users find the registration area in the first place or understand when and why they make the decision to register. Along with the kinds of labeling, error-handling, and other usability problems you would find using the system-focused approach, you could also identify some of the larger issues that affect the site's usefulness. Do users perceive a "call to action" on their own that prompts them to register voluntarily? Do they know what benefits registration would bring?

For example, during a recent test of a major online cosmetics site, our first draft of a test script was a traditional feature-focused set of tasks designed to test key site functionality. But instead, we decided to employ a combined user-focused and scenario-focused test script. Thus, for our first task, we gave participants $50 each and asked them to actually spend the money on the site however they wanted. We carefully recruited people who were representative site users and who already enjoyed buying cosmetics. The results were amazing. As we observed the consternation on participants' faces, and watched them move through the site looking for items they wanted to purchase, we realized that the tasks we had considered assigning in our first draft would not have provided us with as much useful information. In fact, most of the tasks we'd planned to assign (find product X and put it in your shopping cart, or find your boyfriend a fragrance gift) would have resulted in inflated task success. But when users were actually spending money and pursuing their own goals, everything changed. Elements of the site design that had seemed acceptable suddenly became critical to users, like the size of the color palettes used to show lipstick options and the format of the search results (users wanted to see thumbnail images of the products along with text descriptions). By writing a test script that allowed users to set their own goals, we learned a great deal more than we would have by "directing" all the action. The clients were very happy with what was discovered.

In the real world, choosing what to test becomes a balancing act. Clients and designers will sometimes direct us to prompt users to interact with specific modules and sections, and we do so. However, tasks that allow users some flexibility to interact with multiple navigational elements and make choices about which features or content to focus on or ignore give us a much better idea of how the site succeeds under more realistic conditions.

The Pilot Test—or the Dress Rehearsal

Before we actually conduct our usability test, we do a **pilot test**—that is, a run-through with a volunteer test participant. The run-through allows us to evaluate how long the test script is and whether our scenarios can be completed in a reasonable amount of time. It also gives us an opportunity to fine-tune our script to make sure that users are interacting with the right sections of the site in a way that gives us the information we need in order to improve our prototype. As you are finishing a draft of your test script, check the following issues:

- Are the test tasks specific enough that the participants and moderator will know when each task is complete?
- Are the tasks concrete enough that they will generate meaningful results even when performed by different users?
- Have you tested the script to make sure the test will fit into the time allotted?
- Are the task descriptions clear, so that users will know what they are expected to do?
- Are the test tasks sufficiently representative of what users will need and want to be able to do with the site?

- Does your test script match your goals for the test? In other words, will the test allow you to collect the data you need based on your test goals?
- Is the first task simple, so that users start with a positive experience?
- Does the final task provide some degree of closure?

Selecting and Recruiting Test Participants

Testing with representative users is a key factor in getting valid findings. In the professional world, we usually write a **screener** (see Example 6.2), a document that includes a series of questions designed to help us identify test participants who match the website's target user groups. We usually give this screener to a recruiting firm that handles the mechanics of finding and scheduling participants. Sometimes the type of user we want to test is so specific that we have to rely on our clients to recruit participants.

For example, if we were working with a major investment firm and part of its website was designed for its own analysts, we would probably rely on our client to select participants. This is a bit scary, because clients who are sponsoring new website initiatives sometimes recruit people whom they know well. It is important to avoid using test participants who are familiar with the website development project or are invested in its success. You're a lot more likely to get an objective opinion about the prototype from an unbiased observer than from the project sponsor's best friend.

For the purposes of this book, the user groups that you will recruit for your test map back to the personas that you created. You developed a rich understanding of your users by observing them in their environment in Chapter 2. But we also want you to be familiar with how usability testing might work if your involvement in the development process were limited to usability testing. In the professional world, most of your clients will already have a sense of the different groups of users they are trying to support with their website. These groups are usually divided through a process called **market segmentation.** An example of market/user segmentation for a wireless company's website might look like this:

Safety Sally

- In her sixties, on a fixed budget, uses the phone 30 minutes per month or less, strictly for emergencies, spends $20 per month. No one has her number; she doesn't even know her own number.
- Justification: Phone provides safety.

Convenience Carl

- In his thirties, uses the phone 250 minutes per month, calls spouse to say he's late for dinner, has one or two children, mostly makes outbound calls except for family.
- Justification: Phone provides convenience and safety.

Example 6.2: Simplified Screener

Note: The text in all capital letters is not read aloud by the recruiter.

Hello, my name is _____, and I am calling on behalf of _____ Consulting. We're not selling anything. We are looking for consumers to try out the design of an Internet website and would like to see if you might be able to participate. Is this is a convenient time to talk?

1. Do you or does anyone in your household work in advertising or public relations, market research, skin care, or beauty care?

   ❏ Yes   TERMINATE
   ❏ No   CONTINUE

2. Do you or does anyone in your household currently work, or have you or has anyone in your household ever worked, at a Web design agency or in the Internet industry?

   ❏ Yes   TERMINATE
   ❏ No   CONTINUE

3. Excluding e-mail, how much time do you spend on the Web per week?

   ❏ Less than two hours   TERMINATE
   ❏ More than two hours   CONTINUE

4. Have you purchased merchandise on the Web in the last six months?

   ❏ Yes   CONTINUE
   ❏ No   TERMINATE

5. Have you participated in a market research focus group, an in-depth interview, or a usability test in the past six months?

   ❏ Yes   TERMINATE
   ❏ No   CONTINUE

6. Which of the following best describes your household income?

   ❏ Under $30,000   TERMINATE
   ❏ $30,001–$50,000   CONTINUE
   ❏ $50,001–$75,000   CONTINUE
   ❏ $75,001–$100,000   CONTINUE
   ❏ $100,001–$150,000   CONTINUE
   ❏ More than $150,000   CONTINUE

7. What is your occupation?

   RECRUIT A MIX FOR EACH ROUND OF TESTS.

8. Which of the following best describes your highest level of education?

   - ❏ Some high school   TERMINATE
   - ❏ High school graduate   CONTINUE
   - ❏ Some college   CONTINUE
   - ❏ College graduate   CONTINUE
   - ❏ Postgraduate work   CONTINUE

   RECRUIT A MIX.

9. Do you have Internet access at home or at work?

   - ❏ Yes   CONTINUE
   - ❏ No   TERMINATE

10. What brands of cosmetics (both makeup and skin-care) do you use most often?

    ALL MUST MENTION AT LEAST TWO BRANDS ON THE LIST.

11. What type of store do you most often shop in when purchasing cosmetics (skin-care and makeup)?

    - ❏ Drugstore, convenience store   TERMINATE
    - ❏ Specialty store (like Sephora)   CONTINUE
    - ❏ Department store   CONTINUE
      (like Bloomingdale's, Saks Fifth Avenue, Barneys)

12. Which of the following statements describes how you feel about shopping for cosmetics?

    - ❏ I consider shopping for cosmetics a chore—something I need to do, but it isn't any fun.   TERMINATE
    - ❏ I don't mind shopping for cosmetics—but I can't take much time for browsing. I'm just too busy.   TIME-PRESSED QUOTA
    - ❏ I love checking out new cosmetics. I could spend a lot of time in a cosmetics department or a store like Sephora browsing and checking out new products.   GLAMOURAMA QUOTA

13. Which of the following best describes how you approach purchasing cosmetics?

    - ❏ I have a few products that I've been using for a while. I rarely try anything new.   TERMINATE
    - ❏ I have a few products that I stick with, but I like to experiment with something new every now and then.   CONTINUE
    - ❏ I love trying new products; I see what the trend is and experiment a lot.   CONTINUE

14. This last question is just for fun. If you were to win the lottery this week, where would you travel, whom would you bring with you, and why?

THE ANSWER MUST BE ARTICULATE.
EXPLAIN INCENTIVES. (Single-session participants: $75.)
SAY THAT THE TEST WILL BE OBSERVED AND VIDEOTAPED.
GIVE LOCATION OF THE TEST AND DIRECTIONS.

Lifeline Lisa

- A minute "burner," uses 1,500 minutes a month, possibly in sales, uses phone for work and personal purposes, spends $150 per month, switching costs high, makes both inbound and outbound calls. Lots of people have her number.
- Justification: Phone is a lifeline.

Prepay Pete

- Eighteen years old with no credit, got a prepaid phone because he didn't want to pay a deposit or has bad credit, spends lots of time on the phone, spends $30–$60 per month.
- Justification: Phone is a fashion statement.

When you move into your professional career, you'll need to compromise with marketing executives and others to make sure that the key target segments for your site are represented in your usability tests. As you choose whom to recruit, you'll balance the user goals that you discovered from your user research with the business, branding, and technical goals and other constraints that you identified.

Work to select people with the right background and experience by considering the following characteristics:

- *Job-related:* experience level, educational level, degree and kind of prior training
- *Personal:* age, gender, physical differences
- *Location-related:* wage differences, cultural or ethnic factors, physical environment
- *Language-related:* language skills, terminology differences, translation issues
- *Computer/Web-related:* operating systems, facility with the mouse, experience on the Web

We suggest that you conduct your usability tests with about six users. Nielsen and Landauer's frequently quoted 1993 study suggests that even a small number of users can help you find the majority of usability problems. Some have challenged those findings, particularly when large sites with many interactions

need to be tested. Sometimes, with large, complex sites, we do two days of testing and double the number of users to twelve or more. However, for most projects for which budgets and timelines are tight, we feel we can get valuable results
with only six to eight users.

The last thing we want to say about screeners is that, as the name suggests,
they're used to screen possible participants out. Therefore, our recruiters need
something to draw people into agreeing or even wanting to participate in our
study in the first place. People who agree to participate in one of our tests receive an incentive—usually cash. In a classroom or not-for-profit setting, you
may not have a budget for incentives. However, you can be creative and provide
coupons or even food. Obviously, in a classroom setting, you're not going to be
using cash incentives, so do whatever you can to get the right people to participate, and insofar as possible, avoid using friends or people who won't be able to
give you objective responses.

Preparing the Test Materials and Setting Up the Testing Environment

You will normally need to have test participants sign a release form, giving you
permission to record the test and use the results. We also use the release form to
remind participants that we promise to protect them by keeping the results anony-
mous and that they can withdraw from the test at any time. (See the feature "Informed Consent" for suggestions about consent and release forms.) In some
cases, you may also need participants to sign a nondisclosure form, saying that
they will not discuss your (or your client's) prototype with anyone after the test.

You may also want to create a pre- or posttest questionnaire, to gather additional information from the respondents about their experience. We discuss
posttest questionnaires in the subsection on debriefing.

The setup for a usability test can be as simple or complicated as you want to
make it. When we test, we sometimes have a usability lab with remote-control
cameras, a scan converter, digital picture-in-picture, wireless microphones, digital video recording, and an observation room with a one-way mirror where we
can invite clients and design team members to come and observe the test.

But as Jared Spool and the people of User Interface Engineering (UIE) have
reminded us, all you really need is a conference room (see Figure 6.1). In fact, UIE
did some interesting work on an antiques website in a tent at an antiques fair.

What you need to be prepared for is the basics:

- Do you have access to your prototype in either paper or interactive form?
- Are all the website pages that support the scenarios in your test script designed and ready to be viewed?
- Have you prepared any release forms or questionnaires you will need during the test?
- Do you have a way to capture your results, even if it's just a couple of observers dedicated to note-taking?

Informed Consent

Important: Contact your university office of research services before conducting any human-subject research. The following information is presented for reference purposes only.

Use of Audio and Video Recording

For projects in which you intend to make audio and/or video recordings of subjects, your consent form should explain who will have access to the tapes, security measures you will take to protect the privacy of subjects recorded, and what you will do with the tapes upon completion of your project (such as erase them or retain them for future research).

Payment to Subjects

Please note that payment schemes have the potential to be coercive.

Informed-Consent Form

If you are obtaining written informed consent, a copy of the consent form that will be used in the research should be available to all parties concerned (subjects, researcher, client, and so forth). According to the federal code of regulations (45 CFR 46), for university-sponsored research, the consent form must include the following items, when appropriate and applicable:

• A statement of the purpose of the research and a brief description of procedures to be followed.

• A description of any reasonably foreseeable discomforts or risks (psychological, sociological, or physical) to the subjects. If more than minimal risk is involved in the project, a statement concerning your state's Tort Claims Act should be included. Minimal risk means that the probability and magnitude of harm or discomfort anticipated in the research are not greater in and of themselves than those ordinarily encountered in daily life or during the performance of routine physical or psychological examinations or tests.

• A description of any benefits for the subjects or others that may reasonably be expected from the research.

• A statement that participation is voluntary. This should include an assurance that participation may be discontinued at any time and that refusal to participate in, or withdrawal from participation in, the project will result in no penalty or loss of benefits to which the subject is otherwise entitled.

• A statement describing the extent (if any) to which the confidentiality of records through which the subject can be identified will be protected.

• An indication of the commitment in time required to participate in the study.

• An offer to answer any inquiries concerning the project and information concerning whom to contact in case questions arise after the data-collection session is completed. This is usually done by providing the name of the researcher, the client affiliation, and the telephone number(s) on the consent form.

• Signatures:

    • The subject's signature, if appropriate (that is, if the subject is of legal age and is competent to understand and provide informed consent). If individuals who are not of legal age (under the age of eighteen) may inadvertently be recruited for participation in the project, the following statement should appear below the signature:

      "With my signature, I affirm that I am at least eighteen years of age."

    • If the subject's signature is not appropriate, the signature of the parent or guardian (again, if parent or guardian is of legal age) and the name of the subject.

> - An affirmation under the signature stating. "With my signature, I acknowledge that I have received a copy of this consent form to keep."
>
> **Assent Procedures**
>
> In research with children or other participants for whom the ability to give informed consent is otherwise compromised, it is usually appropriate to obtain some form of agreement, or "assent," to participation in the data-collection sessions. For example, even though children or individuals with developmental disabilities cannot formally provide informed consent for participation in research, a researcher should still describe the procedures in language that the subjects can understand and obtain their verbal "agreement" to participate.

- Do test participants know where to meet you?
- Do you have a schedule set up so that test participants arrive at regular intervals? Are any people you want to observe the test able to make it on the day you've scheduled?
- Are the all-important incentives ready, even if they are just chocolate-chip cookies?

Conducting the Test

In this subsection, we talk about how to be an effective moderator, how to record your data, and how to end the test by **debriefing** the test respondents.

Being an Effective Moderator

If making sure that a usability test has been designed properly is the most important factor that affects the value of the testing experience, the next most important factor is the moderator. Ability as a moderator is part aptitude and part experience. Good moderators are good listeners. They don't go into a test session

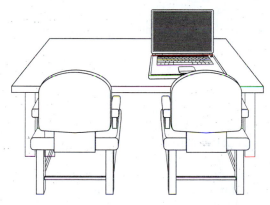

FIGURE 6.1   Typical Conference Room Usability Test Configuration

already convinced that they know what users do or what users want. They do a good job of letting users reveal what they are thinking, not talking over the participants. As we like to say, "Good moderating is about knowing how to shut up." The way you moderate the test, assign tasks, probe for more information, and give off nonverbal signals to the test participants can have a huge effect on the validity of what you learn about your prototype.

Some test participants provide very subtle feedback about what they are experiencing or feeling, and you can't rely only on what they say. The ability to build very quick rapport with participants is key. If the participants don't feel at ease, they may not behave normally and can even provide misleading results. Some participants want a lot of reassurance and handholding, and others want to get right down to business. The moderator must have the ability to sense the participants' needs and adjust the moderating style quickly and accurately.

After you've done your first usability test, you'll probably agree with us that it can be a long day. The moderator has to be the kind of person who can maintain a high level of interest and focus for the entire day and still be a "people person." Often, the findings and flow of a usability test session do not go as planned. The moderator must be very flexible and comfortable with paradox and ambiguity. When moderators are too rigid about the test plan, don't "click" with participants, seem too intimidating, or jump to conclusions, they can undermine the value of a test.

Your ability as a moderator will grow with experience. Just be as sensitive as you can to how you interact with participants.

Doing It Right

When the day of your usability test arrives, you will already have prepared your test script and the materials you need for the test. You will also have already done a "run-through" of the test with a sample user (perhaps a friend) so you will know how long it will take. Relax. When participants arrive, greet them warmly and perhaps use some humor to put them at ease. Offer some refreshment and keep things light. In some cases, you may need to ask them to sign a nondisclosure form or a release form if you are going to videotape. Keep things very informal and use the "housekeeping" time to build rapport and let participants get used to their surroundings.

If observers will be in the room with the participants, introduce them. Explain their role and make the participants feel as comfortable as possible. Make sure that everything you do with your voice and your body language communicates to the participants that your focus is not on them and their performance but rather on the interface and on how well *it* performs in meeting their human needs. Make them your partners in revealing the usability of the interface. Treat them with respect and clearly communicate through your actions as well as your words that *you* need *them* to help you improve your prototype. Validate the professional skills of the users, if appropriate. Assure them that you will be grateful for any difficulties they experience because those difficulties will help you identify elements that need improvement. (See the accompanying feature "Tips for Beginning Your Test.")

After users have had a chance to become familiar with the environment, have them take a seat in front of the computer. As we mentioned when describing the iterative test, we often use a **think-aloud protocol**—a method whereby participants do a verbal stream of consciousness so we know what they are looking at and thinking during the test. Although having to say everything you think obviously slows you down, we make sure that all the tests are conducted under the same conditions, and this method does allow us to measure relative improvement from one version of the prototype to the next.

Helping participants feel comfortable with the think-aloud protocol takes a minute and should be handled carefully. Sometimes we sit at the computer first and go to amazon.com or cnn.com and model the protocol, thinking aloud about exactly what we see and why we choose what we choose. We do it for a minute or so, and then we invite the participants to do the think-aloud on the same site we just used so they can mimic us. Our goal is for them to get comfortable with thinking aloud before we begin the test. It may still be necessary to prompt users to think out loud during the test by asking them, "What are you thinking now?" If users ask a question about an action, the moderator can reply, "What do you think will happen if you do that?"

Some usability professionals prefer to have participants read the tasks themselves. We don't do this because we like the flexibility of being able to modify

---

Tips for Beginning Your Test

The following suggestions are adapted from Jakob Nielsen (1993, 188-90) and Mitchell Gass.

- Explain that the purpose of the test is to evaluate the site, not the test participants.
- Explain that the testing team did not design the site, so participants can speak freely; members of the testing team won't feel bad.
- Explain that the purpose of the test is to generate ideas for improving the design of the site, although you won't be the one who implements the changes.
- Explain that participants can stop the test at any time.
- Assure participants that the results of the test will be confidential.
- Explain any recording devices being used.
- Invite participants to ask questions before the test begins.
- Encourage participants to ask questions during the test (say that you want to know about anything they find unclear), but explain that you won't actually be answering their questions until after the test, since the goal of the test is to assess the site on its own merits, without any additional explanations.
- Provide any relevant instructions. (For example, tell participants to think out loud. If you are testing how fast the site can be used, tell participants to try to work as quickly as possible.)
- Explain that you want to know how the site works for the participants, not how they think it will work for other people.

the tasks if we are doing one of our more informal iterative tests. Sometimes, if you are working on a very early prototype, you might need to summarize some parts of the interaction verbally because certain portions of the website are either not yet created or not completed or not yet fully functional. Obviously, how effectively you can do that will play a large part in how well the test goes.

Participants will often ask you what they should do or whether they've done something correctly. Remain neutral in every way so they can decide what they should do and how they feel. Carefully turn questions back to participants so you can understand what their expectations were rather than giving them the "right answers." A common problem for moderators is asking leading questions or saying things that suggest to users, however subtly, what you would like them to do or what the "right answer" is. Never show surprise at what users are doing; merely encourage them to think aloud about their process. One of the most difficult parts of moderating a test is knowing when and how to probe for more information and when to refrain from doing so. It's important to keep an even voice and control your body language so that all of your attention and emphasis is on the interface.

Occasionally, when users have failed a task, you must prompt them to abandon the task, return to the homepage, or begin the task again with a better understanding of what they're trying to do. Use your best powers of judgment and observation to determine whether participants have truly abandoned the task or have become so frustrated that it is necessary for you to step in and move to the next scenario.

Capturing Data

The most foolproof method we've discovered for capturing data from usability tests is video. We swear by it. No matter how experienced usability professionals are, they will still miss important things during a test. And trying to moderate and take notes at the same time almost guarantees that you will focus on the most obvious problems and not have the time or mental bandwidth to notice the more subtle issues, which may be far more important. Although there are numerous studies that recount the limitations of memory, it always shocks us to meet Ph.D. usability consultants who try to write usability test reports based on memory or from their hastily taken notes. Cameras are data-capture devices. They don't make decisions about what is important and what isn't. They get everything within their field of view. Earlier we mentioned that you don't need lots of equipment or an expensive lab to do testing—and that's true. New programs like Camtasia make it possible to capture "video" of your usability test with only a PC and a microphone (see the accompanying feature). Whether on digital videotape or directly on your hard drive, we strongly recommend that you capture your usability sessions.

If you are going to be partly dependent on your notes to record your usability test, try to have multiple note takers, since different observers will notice different things. Practice taking notes before your first actual test. You want to record everything you possibly can—what respondents say and what they do. You even want to record any facial expressions that suggest their reactions to the interface. To take good notes, however, you must learn to differentiate between what respondents actually say and do and what you *think* they are feeling or thinking. It's all too easy to supply your own interpretation of what you see. Don't do it. A good practice is to write down what you see and hear in one column and record any ideas about what you think your observations mean in another column. When possible, ask respondents what they are thinking if you see potentially significant body language or facial expressions.

Debriefing

After participants have finished carrying out the scenarios in the test script, you have the opportu-

---

An Alternative to Video: Camtasia

An elegant solution for usability data capture is Camtasia, a new computer program made in Michigan by a company called TechSmith. Unfortunately, it is only available on the PC platform; however, it is very simple and effective.

Camtasia records what is happening on the screen directly to a computer's hard drive, and by plugging in a simple microphone, you can get perfect-resolution "videos" of where users go and what they click on, and have a soundtrack of their think-aloud comments and questions.

If you use Camtasia's default settings, an hourlong usability session results in about a 200-megabyte file, so make sure there is room on your computer to save something that big. Also, in record mode, Camtasia slows down even very fast computers, so you might need to run it on a fairly new machine in one of your campus computer labs.

All in all, this method is extremely portable: the only things you need are a laptop and the best microphone you can afford. It's also very easy to scan through sessions later and look for specific incidents. You can download a free thirty-day trial version of Camtasia at www.techsmith.com.

---

nity to debrief them about what they did and probe more deeply regarding problems that you observed but didn't want to stop the test to discuss. Start by allowing respondents to talk about what is on their mind. They may have important feedback about specific tasks and problems they encountered that you might have missed. If observers are in the room, they may ask questions during debriefing, but only when the moderator calls on them. If observers are in another room watching through a one-way mirror, they can write down questions for the moderator to ask. We talked earlier about how asking users what they *would* like or what they *would* do generally leads to unreliable data. However, after participants have had some time to interact with a prototype, their preference statements can be much more interesting and insightful. Thus, we recommend that you take the opportunity to talk to participants about what happened in the test.

Transforming Data into Findings and Recommendations

To maximize your efficiency, start organizing your data while the test is still under way. If, by the end of your usability test, you already have some key notes about important events, errors, or other issues from each test session, they will give you a head start on your data analysis.

Using the Highlighter Method

We like to keep printouts of screen shots (or photocopies if we are using a paper prototype) on hand during and after usability testing. Then, after each test session, we take a highlighter and highlight on paper any controls or areas where we observed a usability problem, and we jot a few quick notes about what we observed. We do not recommend doing a "rush job" of reporting results, because often by the end of a usability test, your brain is pretty fried. It is easy to make snap assessments that turn out to be wrong after you've spent more time with the data. However, one of the realities of our professional life is that teams often need immediate feedback about critical findings and/or recommendations. The highlighter method enables us to identify all of the major usability problems we've observed by the end of the day. Then we can send the development team an e-mail pinpointing the most serious usability problems. We always make it very clear, though, that those first-blush reactions are preliminary, and we reserve the right to change them after we've had a chance to review the data more thoroughly.

Watching the Tapes

There is little point in videotaping, or using Camtasia to capture your usability evaluations, if you are then going to make judgments from memory without bothering to watch the sessions. Even the most experienced researchers miss important data during a test. There's simply no way you can remember more than a fraction of what you saw during eight or more hours of testing. So watch your sessions!

Observing the sessions later in a quiet setting where you have time to pause and reflect on subtle things you may have missed can provide very important insights. Of course, the frustrating thing about watching the tapes is that you can't pause and ask respondents follow-up questions. However, we've taken to asking our test participants for their e-mail addresses so that we can send them follow-up questions. We've found that people are actually very interested in helping and love to stay involved and watch how an interface improves over time. We realize that it can be very hard to find the time to watch five to six hours or more of videotape. However, we feel that the return on investment is very high in terms of catching more subtle, but no less severe, usability problems and/or insights about users.

Recording Success Rates

A simple table can help us assemble task-success numbers from our usability test. During the test, we record right on the test plan whether or not users were successful in accomplishing the tasks assigned. In some cases, it is useful to set a

PROFESSIONAL PROFILE *Kara Pernice Coyne*

Watching the Video
Kara Pernice Coyne

Director of Research, Nielsen-Norman Group

People have actually laughed at me when I told them I watched usability videotapes. Others have said it's just not worth the time. Still others said they think it could be valuable, but it is just too time-consuming or boring. One quote comes to mind: "It's like watching paint dry." I will not argue that it is completely exciting, but that does not make it any less valuable. Even the best usability professionals and teams of designers miss issues during studies.

People talk when observing sessions. They get excited. Sometimes they start redesigning then and there. Especially in those cases, people just plain miss stuff. Watching tapes can help you see some of the more subtle issues users encountered. Also, sometimes due to schedule conflicts, people don't make the sessions, so watching the video as a group can be invaluable.

At Lotus, sometimes we'd just play videos at lunch, and people would eat and watch. We'd pause the tape and discuss incidents. This activity led to a lot of insights and was even team-building. There's a reason why the NFL has instant replay—not just for questionable calls but also to revel in remarkable plays or interesting ones. There's no reason you can't do the same when developing software—just fewer broken bones here.

The four most important reasons I recommend watching videos are to:

1. See things you missed.
2. Play different sessions at different points to demonstrate patterns.
3. Remind the development team of issues, usable designs, and design improvements as a product's design iterates and across multiple product releases.
4. Review competitive designs against your own.

time benchmark for task success—for example, when users are unable to check out successfully using their shopping cart within seven minutes. Depending on the needs of our audience and the relevance of the data, we might report different kinds of errors—errors committed that users were able to recover from, those that users could not recover from, and tasks that users were ultimately able to succeed at, but only after far exceeding the benchmark (for example, users who found the 800 number, but only after ten minutes of anxious searching).

Recording Time on Task

You don't have to be a math whiz to report user performance data, because all you need is simple descriptive statistics—mean, median, and range. Start with the **mean**—that is, the average of all the numbers. The mean will give you a fuzzy picture of how users performed overall. Calculate the mean using this formula:

$$\text{mean} = \frac{\text{sum of individual users' completion times}}{\text{number of participants}}$$

If you are comparing results with data from an earlier test—maybe a pretest from before a site's redesign—you are obviously interested in seeing whether users performed better or worse. Watch out, though, if there is a wide variation among the times. For example, if you had five users try task 1 and the first four all took about 2 minutes and the last user took something like 9 minutes, then your mean, or the average of 3.4 minutes, is probably not the number most reflective of user performance.

In that case, you would use the median. The median time it took users to do a task is exactly in the middle of all the times if they are listed in descending order. In this case, the median would be two minutes.

Identifying Repeat Offenders

The next step in our data analysis is to identify what we call the repeat offenders. We examine our highlighter-marked printouts. We look at our success rates and task times, and we identify those tasks that produced frequent errors. We concentrate on those tasks and go back to the video and watch them again. We review our notes, and we begin to focus on the controls, elements, labels, and content that users needed to notice, manipulate, or modify in order to achieve their goals. We also focus on errors that users made and again try to notice those that repeat. Then we begin looking for connections between the errors and the design. Before long, we are able to track down the offending elements of the interface. This error-analysis process can be tedious, but it is crucial. We recommend that you conduct your error analysis over a period of several days.

Prioritizing Problems and Rating Them by Severity

Once we have made a list of usability problems, we then proceed to rate the problems in terms of their severity. Our ranking is based on the typical user's ability to complete the tasks, assuming that the technology itself works correctly and that errors are caused by the interface design. The severity ranking is also based on the relative frequency with which users encounter the issue. A given issue will be considered less severe if it is encountered infrequently than if it is encountered more frequently. Here's how we categorize usability observations:

- *Major:* These problems are the most critical because they involve users' being unable to complete their task correctly. A common example of this type of error would be if users simply could not determine which control, information, or sequence is necessary to perform the task.

Websites should never be delivered with any critical-level errors.

- *Moderate:* These problems caused significant difficulties for users. A common example of this type of error would be using the wrong control or using the right control incorrectly.

  Errors of this sort typically account for a high incidence of support requests.

- *Minor:* These nuisance-level problems hampered users during their performance of the task. Examples include users' having trouble finding the correct command or controls to complete the task.

  Minor errors leave users frustrated and dissatisfied with the website.

- *Good*: An object is well-designed.

Creating Recommendations

Remember that quote from Jeffrey Rubin about the doctor? That the value of doctors doesn't lie only in how well they can gather data like heart rate, blood pressure, and so forth but in what they learn from that data? Obviously, if your website is sick, you want more than a detailed report about how sick it is; you want to know how to make it well.

If you are using these methods to improve the prototype you've developed for this class, then you are obviously the one who designed the website, the one who has the decision-making authority to make changes and improvements, as well as the one who will have to spend time implementing those changes. That's not always the case.

In the professional world—where you could be working as an information architect, a content strategist, a technical writer, or a usability consultant—you may not have the authority to make final decisions about changes. Your job may only be to evaluate the usability of the interface while others decide how they are going to solve the usability problems you find. However, if we are hired to do a usability test, we always make recommendations about how to resolve the problems we've found.

What you recommend should be grounded in what you observed during the test. For example, during a recent test of a consumer health-care product site, Michael's team had several scenarios that involved finding dosage information. Obviously, this was a "known-item" search; users knew the name of the product that they already owned as well as the exact information for which they were looking. After identifying the task as one that had high time-on-task numbers coupled with a low success rate, the team examined it more closely.

After looking at the videotape, Michael observed that the information architecture of the site was set up according to symptom. Users who were looking for dosage information for a popular children's medicine first had to figure out which symptom it treated and click on the name of the symptom before they could confirm that they had found the right product. To find the dosage infor-mation, users then had to select "How to take ProductName." Most users were unable to translate "How to take ProductName" into their mental image of what they were looking for, which was dosage information. Our recommenda-tions were: first, augment the symptom-based navigation and information ar-chitecture with a product-based model; second, simplify "Which Product to Take" and provide a clear navigation bar on each product page that included the more obvious "Dosage Chart" as a choice. After testing a prototype with these changes applied, we saw a 40 percent increase in the success rate and a massive drop in time on task.

Sometimes the solutions to usability problems you identify are not this obvi-ous. After you spend time reviewing the video, take a day off from the project. Think about what you saw users trying to accomplish. Carefully consider the objects, links, and areas they chose in error. You may discover clues about what went wrong that can guide you to design something that will help users succeed.

In the professional world, the kinds of recommendations you make for solv-ing the usability problems you identify will depend on a few political factors as well as organizational issues. Typically, you're getting paid for your work, which means you have a professional obligation to find problems, report them accurately, and make good recommendations. But clients won't pay you to make them feel stupid, so you'll need to be positive and tactful in your recom-mendations, and the more you know about the clients and the stakeholders in the development process, the more effective you will be in sharing your results.

Presenting Results

The way we present usability findings has evolved over the years. And we've seen more than one effective method. Some usability and research companies deliver their reports in PowerPoint. They usually have lots of screen shots with lines leading from the unusable areas to paragraphs of text that explain problems and make recommendations. We've also seen more narrative textual reports that are sprinkled with small visual examples and recommendations.

We've settled on a report format that combines these two approaches and functions more like a punch list (see Example 6.3). This is the format used by the technical and project management community to track and resolve "bugs" dur-ing the quality assurance (QA) phase of the development process. Although we certainly don't want usability testing to be interpreted as something that is only done during what software folks like to call user acceptance testing (UAT), just before launch, we do like people to regard usability problems as being as im-portant as fixing technical bugs. We also find that the chart-style format with a brief executive summary lends itself to being scanned and referenced easily. Here is an outline of the major sections we include:

Executive summary
Description of test methodology and test circumstances

Participant list
Task list
Results
Appendixes (test script and other test materials)

Whichever format you choose, make sure that as you create major sections, you provide readers with clear access to points of interest and a clear road map to the structure of the document. Use headings and other document design elements to give the document cohesion and to direct readers' attention to key elements of the report. For example, you might let each major insight into the site's usability serve as a heading for a list of observations that support that insight. Remember that clarity in document design means that you must signal the purpose of each textual element clearly, make the document's logical structure as transparent as possible, and help readers not only to understand each piece of information but to grasp and properly evaluate both its importance and its relationship to the rest of the document.

Remember also that the visual arrangement and physical structure of the document or presentation signify meaning, relationships of power, connections, and so forth. Think about the rhetorical implications of your choices, the quality of the materials, the presence or absence of color, and the way in which the text is to be consumed (turning pages, listening to a presentation, viewing a multimedia presentation). Each choice communicates assumptions about your audience, about the importance of the information you're providing, and about the relationship between your test team and the decision-making audience.

Video Summary of Findings

Our written reports are sometimes accompanied by a highlights video. There is nothing more frustrating than watching reports from usability tests sit on the

NameCo.com				
Object	**Observation**		**Level**	**Recommendation**
11 Missing dHTML navigation on home-page	DHTML navigation allows greater information architecture transparency. However, the dHTML navigation as currently implemented only works below the home page. One user who had found the coverage area lower in the site structure using dHTML tried to find it again from the home page and could not: about us | products & services | cu calling plans wireless data service coverage area promotions The dHTML intra-section secondary nav only works for that section. We observed several users mousing over customer service from within the products and services section trying to make the DHTML secondary nav appear. This partial implementation violates conventions users have learned elsewhere on the web.		Moderate	Apply dHTML consistently throughout the IA structure—Home, secondary, tertiary

FIGURE 6.2 Sample Page from Usability Test Results

shelf collecting dust while development teams and executives work from their own assumptions without understanding their actual users.

If few usability professionals actually take the time to watch video to analyze their data, even fewer edit their tapes and produce stand-alone video reports. However, by using simple video-editing software like iMovie, or the editor that comes with Camtasia, we can produce videos that are much harder to ignore than a PowerPoint presentation or a fifty-page usability report.

When we began our careers, we were satisfied to be doing tests with real users and finding problems in our own and others' websites. Now, we realize that our work is in vain when political or other obstacles within the organizations we serve prevent usability problems' actually being resolved.

Of course, the best way to create consensus is to have all the stakeholders attend the test in person. But the reality is that you are never going to manage to involve all of them. Sometimes the people we most need to persuade with user understanding are those who are the most skeptical of our methods and findings—and they're not about to give up a lunch hour, an evening, or an entire day to watch a usability test.

Done right, video summaries of usability research, organized and divided by simple title text and fade-to-black, with some basic voice narration, can allow our clients to have a "vicarious experience" with users and give them detail and conviction about our conclusions. Because they've been given the opportunity to evaluate the data on their own, they are more likely to accept our recommendations.

When we're watching the tapes to analyze our findings, we note the "time stamp" of interesting comments and interactions. We then assemble those clips into our video summary of findings. We've made usability videos with two VCRs doing the pause/record shuffle. And we've taken our tapes to professional editing studios for help in creating very professional productions. Most universities have instructional support labs with publicly accessible video-editing booths. In fact, all Macintosh computers come with Apple's easy-to-use iMovie, allowing you to look like a pro in editing your usability findings. Of course, the fun of creating a video should not sidetrack you from focusing on the validity of your findings. But taking a crack at creating video summaries of your findings can produce a great portfolio piece for demonstrating your capabilities to potential employers.

Ethical Video Editing

Using video to summarize the findings of your usability test requires the highest ethical standards. If your videos manage to carry the "objective observer" narrative voice of a PBS documentary, your objectivity and credibility as a researcher will be preserved. However, both as a student and later as a professional, your credibility will be compromised if a stakeholder attends a day's sessions and then notices that you have selected only those video clips that support your arguments.

Do not give your colleagues or stakeholders any reason to question your ethics. Be extremely careful to show accurately representative task success/ failure with a particular feature or control, so that observers can see user performance, criticism, or praise in the same context as someone who observed the entire day of testing.

The ethics of video editing are actually very similar to the ethics of any reporting or research, written or otherwise. Any written document that reports behavioral research is both summary and commentary on data collection for a specific task or client need. If you make a hasty "buffet" selection of only those pithy quotes and choices that support a skewed argument, your colleagues and stakeholders will not trust you. When you conduct a usability test, be it on a website you've created or on someone else's work, it is your responsibility to set prejudice aside. This can be very difficult when you have invested a great deal of time and effort in building a section of the site that performs very poorly. Hearing users give negative feedback or watching them fail tasks repeatedly in an area of the site that you've labored over for hours can be very discouraging the first time it happens. However, do not make the mistake of conveniently ignoring those video clips or failing to mention the problems in your written report— focusing instead on other areas that you don't feel the need to "protect."

In our academic and professional lives, we have noticed that stakeholders quickly learn whom they can trust. Those who consistently demonstrate high ethical standards in their written and video reporting of usability evaluations are trusted. Make no mistake, creating websites can be a contentious process. There are many competing interests, and turf battles and disagreements are commonplace. However, by earning a reputation as someone who can put personal preference aside and objectively evaluate and report findings from usability evaluations, you will find that stakeholders trust you, and you will be much more successful.

✔ FINAL CHECKLIST

Planning the Test

- Are test tasks sufficiently representative of what users will need and want to be able to do with the site?
- Does your test script match your goals for the test? In other words, will the test allow you to collect the data you need based on your test goals?
- Do test tasks address the business and design concerns of key stakeholders in the site?
- Have you found an appropriate balance between feature-focused tasks and user-focused, exploratory tasks?
- Are the tasks specific enough that participants and the moderator can tell when each task is complete?

- Are the test tasks concrete enough that they will generate meaningful results even when performed by different users?
- Have you prepared all the materials you will need during the test, including the test script, any pretest or posttest questionnaires, release or nondisclosure forms, and so forth?
- Have you identified which metrics you are most interested in, such as success rates or time on task?
- Have you found an appropriate location and time for the test?
- Have you invited key stakeholders to attend the test sessions?

Recruiting Participants

- Have you identified what user groups you need to test?
- Have you tested your screener to make sure it will successfully identify users who fit your target market?
- Have you arranged for participant incentives?

Conducting a Pilot Test

- Have you tested the script to make sure the test will fit into the time allotted?
- Are the task descriptions clear, so that users will know what they are expected to do?
- Have you prepared any supporting materials you'll need for the test, including consent and disclosure forms, questionnaires, visual prompts, and the like?

Conducting Your Test

- Do you have a comfortable environment for your test participants, perhaps including food or soft drinks in the reception area?
- Are you focused on treating your test participants with respect for their expertise and involving them as partners in your test?
- Did you have your participants sign a consent and nondisclosure form?
- Did observers remain quiet and unobtrusive during the test?
- Did the moderator stay warm and friendly, avoiding leading questions or directive body language?
- Did you remember to ask participants for their e-mail address, if desired?

Capturing Your Data

- Do you have access to a video recorder to capture your data?
- Can you record the output of the computer screen?

- Can you make an audio recording of your test sessions?
- Can your observers tell the difference between what they see and what they think about what they see?
- Do you have multiple observers taking notes? Have they practiced capturing both the test participants' comments and the test participants' paths through the site?
- Do you have printouts of the site pages readily available, so that you can mark problem areas with a highlighter during the test?

Analyzing and Reporting Your Results

- Have you identified repeated errors and patterns of errors?
- Have you captured success rates or any other metrics you planned to collect?
- Have you categorized your observations in terms of the severity of the problems observed?
- Have you watched your videotapes carefully?
- Are your recommendations thoughtful and qualified? Have you clearly identified which recommendations need to be validated through further testing?
- If you are creating a video summary of results, have you edited the clips carefully? Have you provided adequate context for each clip and edited out extraneous material?
- Do you provide effective subtitles and/or voice narration?
- Have you included visual transitions, where appropriate?

Ethical Considerations

- Have you reported your results as objectively as possible, avoiding exaggerated claims or misleading information?
- If you are creating a highlights video, do you provide enough context for your clips to make them easy to understand?
- If you have deleted segments from the middle of a clip, have you included a simple transition to signal viewers that time has passed?
- Have you been open to *all* the feedback you received from users?
- Are your recommendations responsible and appropriate?

Quality Control

- Does your usability report look attractive and professional?
- Have you eliminated spelling, punctuation, and syntax errors?
- Have your graphics reproduced well?

 **REFERENCES**

Dumas, Joseph, and Janice Redish. 1999. *A Practical Guide to Usability Testing.* Portland, Oreg.: Intellect.

Krug, Steve. 2000. *Don't Make Me Think: A Common Sense Approach to Web Usability.* Indianapolis, Ind.: Que.

Mayhew, Deborah J. 1999. *The Usability Engineering Lifecycle: A Practitioner's Handbook for User Interface Design.* San Francisco: Morgan Kaufmann.

Nielsen, Jakob. 1994. *Usability Engineering.* San Francisco: Morgan Kaufmann.

Nielsen, Jakob and Thomas K. Landaucr. (1993). "A mathematical model of the finding of usability problems." *Proceedings of INTERCHI 93*, 206-213. New York, NY: ACM

Rubin, Jeffrey. 1994. *Handbook of Usability Testing: How to Plan, Design, and Conduct Effective Tests.* New York: Wiley.

Rubin, Jeffrey. "The Usability Yardstick." http://www.usability.com

Schriver, Karen. 1997. *Dynamics in Document Design: Creating Texts for Readers.* New York: Wiley.

Spool, Jared M. 1998. *Web Site Usability.* San Francisco: Morgan Kaufmann.

Glossary

Balance   the relationship between the size, position, and light/dark qualities of your content items

Benchmark usability test   a test measuring a particular quality of a site or system, usually for comparison with the results from another test, either of a prior or subsequent design of the same site, or with the results of testing a competitor site

Blank space   the space between content elements in your layout

Brand attributes   the supporting benefits the customer receives from the product or service, including functional or emotional benefits

Brand personality   how the brand is expressed, or communicated to customers (through shapes, colors, etc.)

Brand promise   the primary benefit provided to customers that will hopefully differentiate a product or service from the competition

Cascading style sheet   a list specifying the visual appearance, or style, of selected Web page elements such as headings, tables, text, etc.

Categorical order   dividing your content into categories. Categories may be based on topic, task, location, chronology, hierarchy, alphabet, etc.

Continuity   a principle of visual grouping based on touching or being connected by a line

End goal   what the persona expects to achieve using the product or service

Experience goal   how the user wants to feel when using a product, such as having fun or not feeling stupid, or wanting to feel secure when using an online banking site

Flash   a simple program that allows you to create interactive animated features for your website

Grid   a clear pattern of horizontal or vertical lines that are used to organize and group content elements in a layout

Heuristic usability evaluation   an evaluation of a system or site according to accepted usability principles from prior usability research

Information architecture   the structure of your information, as represented by your labels, categorization scheme, navigation, and the relationships between pages

Iterative usability test   a process of testing a design, revising the design, re-testing, and re-designing, in order to make the design more effective and useful

Javascript   a simple programming language that allows you to design interactive features on a website

Life goal   a high-level goal such as "retire by age 45" that may shape user priorities, but which are usually less relevant in design than experience goals or end goals

Logical order   organizing your content as an assertion, support, and a conclusion

Narrative order   organizing your content based on describing a process or occurrence through time

Nomenclature   a system of labels for content chunks, such as the text used in headings, navigation, and links.

Persona   a constructed profile of a "user" representing the behavioral goals of a particular group of users, based on field interviews and observation

Pilot test a run-through of a usability test with a volunteer test participant to make sure that the tasks are achievable and the instructions are clear before formal usability testing begins

Prototype an early version of a website or software system that can be used to evaluate the success of the proposed design

Proximity a principle of visual grouping based on nearness of position

Requirements document a record of what the site owners need, the site users need, and what the design team has agreed to provide

Screener also called a "participant screener," the screener is a series of questions that are used to identify test participants that will match the site's target user groups

Similarity a principle of visual grouping based on similarity of color, shape, or size

Site map a visual representation of how the pages of a website are grouped and linked.

Subject matter expert an expert on a particular content area

Task flow a graphical representation of the inputs, objects, actions, decisions, and results of a process

Test script a series of questions and tasks given to a usability test participant by a moderator

Think-aloud protocol a testing method in which test participants attempt to verbalize what they are thinking during the test in a verbal stream-of-consciousness

Usability the effectiveness, efficiency, and satisfaction associated with a website or software system. Effectiveness is often measured in terms of how accurately and completely users can achieve specified goals. Efficiency is measured in terms of time or effort required to achieve goals. Satisfaction is a subjective measure of the comfort and acceptance users felt while using the system.

Visual design a representation of a page design as it will appear in its final form, with colors and all visual elements

Wireframe a paper or electronic representation of the structure and layout of a single page from a website.

Index

360-degree virtual-reality tour, 21

A
Actions, 124
  consequences, 127
  pages, 69
  user perception. *See* Call to action
Active voice, usage, 11, 109, 112
  example, 113
Adjectives, usage (avoidance), 11
Administrative metadata, 125
Advertising, 124
Alignment, 75
  usage, 75f
Allmusic.com, 56
Alphabet. *See* Location Alphabet Time
  Category Hierarchy
ALT tag, usage, 117, 120, 121
Amazon.com, 153
  site map, example, 57f
  visual design, example, 61f
Animated GIFs, implementation (excess), 121
Appendixes, usage, 161
Apple. *See* iMac
Assent procedures, 151
Asymmetrical balance, 94f
Asymmetry, usage, 92–93
Audience
  defining. *See* Websites
  discussion, 11
  identification. *See* Website owners
  site owner brand, tone/image, 26
  style guide section, 96
Audience-specific categories, 108
Audience-specific conceptualization. *See*
  Categories
Audio recording, usage, 150
Awards, 4

B
Back-end vendors, 55
Balance. *See* Asymmetrical balance; Layout
  point, 92
Banner ads, 71

BBC
  content page, consistency, 89f
  section page, underlying grid, 89f
Behavior patterns, personas (representations),
  43–44
Behavioral goals, 44f
Bell Labs, 135
Benchmark usability test, 139
  formality, 140
Beyer, Hugh, 30, 39, 65
Bias, avoidance, 125
Blank space
  importance, 91–93
  usage, 77, 90–92. *See also* Text
Blinking text, avoidance, 121
Blue, impact, 77
Body language, 104
Body text, 86
  ragged-right margins, usage, 87
BOGSATT. *See* Bunch of guys sitting around
  a table talking
Bold effect, application, 85
Bolded words, 115
Bookmark, difficulty, 119
Brand
  attributes, 23–24
  benefit. *See* Website owner brand
  competition, relationship, 25
  personality, 23–24
  positioning. *See* Website owner brand
  promise, 23–24
  relationship, 25
  strategies, differences, 68f
Brand-positioning statement, 25
Branding, 8
  goals, identification/analysis. *See* Website
  owners
  identification, 25
Bringhurst, Robert, 99
Browser. *See* World Wide Web
Buddhism, philosophy, 136
Buffet selection, disadvantage, 163
Bunch of guys sitting around a table talking
  (BOGSATT), 26–27

Business
  financing, 45f
  goals. *See* Website owners

C
Call to action, user perception, 143
Camtasia, 154, 155
Capital letters, avoidance. *See* Text
Captions, usage, 86
Card sorting, 50–51
  functionality items, usage, 51
  information objects, usage, 51f
Categorical order, 108
Categories. *See* Location Alphabet Time
    Category Hierarchy
  audience-specific conceptualization, 52–53
  conceptualization, 52–53
  creation, 108
  pages, 4
  task-oriented conceptualization, 52
  topical conceptualization, 52
Categorization. *See* Items
Category-overview pages, 69
Cause-and-effect relationships, 137
Chart-style format, usage, 160
Chunks. *See* Information
  content, breaking. See User-focused
    chunks
  focus. *See* Content chunks
  summaries, usage. *See* Content chunks
Click (here) technique, 12
Closed-ended questions, 104
Closure. *See* Usability test tasks
Color
  design tips, 76
  emotional characteristics, 76–77
  impact, 76–77
  saturation, 76
  technical characteristics, 76
  usage, 76
  value, 76
Command-line applications, 28
Communication. *See* Hierarchy; Message;
    Relationships; Technical communi-
    cation
  ethics, 126–128
Comparisons, making, 120
Competition, relationship. *See* Brand
Complementary persona, 43
Components, reuse, 55
Comprehension, reinforcement, 104
Computer
  experience, 148

  interaction. *See* Human-computer
    interaction
  knowledge, 33
  monitors, resolution, 82
Computer-generated wireframes, 7f
Concepts, visualization, 120
Concreteness. *See* Usability test tasks
Concurrent events, 55
Conditional elements, 55
Conference room usability test configuration,
    example, 151f
Connection speed, 33
Connections/paths, 55
Consequences. *See* Actions
Consistency, 69
Content
  accessibility, 92f, 121
  breaking. *See* User-focused chunks
  crafting, 102
  creation, 132. *See also* World Wide Web
    checklist, 129–130
  editing, 128
  effectiveness. *See* Portfolio
    testing, 128
  elements, design, 80–87
  groups, signaling, 75f
  identification, 8
  information
    gathering, 103
    highlighting, 109
  labels. *See* User-centered content labels
  maintenance. *See* User-focused content
  navigation, ease, 124–125
  visual structure, 108–115
Content chunks
  focus, example, 116f
  main points, clarity/usage, 112
  summaries, usage, 109
Context
  headings, impact, 115
  providing. *See* Data
Continuity, 73, 78–79
  examples, 78f
  principles, 93
Contrast, principles, 93
Cooper, Alan, 41, 65
  profile, 42–43
Copyright issues. *See* Photographs
Course descriptions, 4
Coyne, Kara Pernice (profile), 157
Credibility, 14–15
  establishment, 125–126
  increase, 125–126

Credit cards
  information, entering, 47
  request, reason, 48
Cropping, 82
  decisions. *See* Images
Cross-divisional design team, 105
Cross-functional teams, usage, 33–35
Cross-reference links, 60
Customer-centered requirements, creation.
    See Design
Customer-validated requirements, creation.
    See Design
Customers
  profiles, development, 135
Customers, identification. *See* Website owners

D
Data
  capture. *See* Usability tests
  context, providing, 120
  gathering. *See* User-directed data gathering
  organization, 155–156
  transformation. *See* Usability testing;
    Usability tests
  visualization, 120
Data-entry pages, 69
Databases. *See* Relational database
  usage, 3
Davis, Jack, 66, 100
Debriefing. *See* Usability test participants
Decision points, 55
Dell
  home site, example, 67f
  homepage, 109f
Descriptive metadata, 125
Design
  customer-centered requirements, creation,
    135
  customer-validated requirements, creation,
    135
  decisions (capture), style guide usage, 96–
    97
  direction, examples, 84f
  elements, 69
  success, evaluation, 93–94
  team, awareness. *See* Technical limitations
  test, preparation, 97
Detail pages, 69
Digital picture-in-picture, usage, 149
Digital video recording, usage, 149
Direct-marketing sitelettes, 71
Directness, 126
Discount usability, 138–139

Document design, focus, 86
Document/presentation
  physical structure, 161
  visual arrangement, 161
Domain knowledge, 33
Dumas, Joseph C., 28, 39, 166

E
E-business architecture, core components, 36
E-commerce success stories, 49
E-mail
  addresses, 156
  links, usage, 3
Editorial consistency (style guide section), 96
Effectiveness, definition, 133
Efficiency, definition, 133–134
Elements. *See* Visual elements
  reader attention, 11
  reduction, 9
  spacing, 9
Emotional characteristics. *See* Color
Enclosure, usage, 75f
End goals, 45
Environment, utilization. *See* Online envi-
    ronment
Errors, elimination. *See* Grammatical errors
Ethical dilemmas, 127
Ethics, 14–15, 18. *See also* Communication;
    Video editing
  considerations, 130, 165
Evenson, Shelley (profile), 32–33
Executive summary, 160
Experience design, 2–12, 40, 49–61
  checklist, 63–64
Experience goals, 45
Expert reviews, 136
Explanatory text, usage, 120
Exploratory test scripts, 143–144

F
Fade-to-black technique, 162
Fair use. *See* Photographs
Feature-focused test scripts, 140, 142–143
Feedback
  providing, 104, 152
  requirement, 143
Field visit summary, 34f
Figure/ground, relationship, 78–
Figures, interpretation, 79f
Findings/recommendations, 155
  video summary, 161–162
First draft, 132
First-blush reactions, 156

Flash
  animation
    implementation, excess, 121
    usage, example, 123f
  introductory pages, avoidance, 121
  plug-in, installation, 122
Flowcharting application, usage, 53
Follow-up questions, 156
Frames
  avoidance, 121
  usage, 117, 119
Framing, 83–84
Friendliness, 126
Functionality, 8
  (style guide section), 96
  items, usage. *See* Card sorting

G
Garrett, Jesse James, 55
Gass, Mitchell, 153
Gates, Bill, 42
Geometric forms, usage, 9
Gestalt
  definition, 72
  principles. *See* Visual grouping
  psychologists, 78
  theory, 73
Google
  approach, 55
  homepage, example, 56f
Grammatical errors, elimination, 128
Graphic consistency (style guide
    section), 96
Graphical user interface (GUI), 28
Graphics, 80–81, 130
  inclusion. *See* Informational images/
    graphics
Greeked text, 59
Green, impact, 77
Grid, usage, 77, 90, 92f. *See also* Layout
Ground, relationship. *See* Figure/ground
Grouped pages, 55
Growth goals, identification, 22–23
GUI. *See* Graphical user interface

H
Hackos, JoAnn T., 39
Headings. *See* Titles/headings
  impact. *See* Context
  usage, 11, 109, 113–114. *See also* Sub-
    headings
Heuristic evaluations, contrast. *See* Usability
  tests

Heuristic usability evaluations, 136
Hierarchical relationships, 73
Hierarchy, 53. *See also* Location Alphabet
    Time Category Hierarchy
  communication, 74, 88
Highlighter method, usage, 156
Holtzblatt, Karen, 30, 39, 65
Homepages, 498
  design, 94–95
    effectiveness, 95f
  information, placement, 94
  wireframe, creation, 59
Honesty, degree, 127
Horizontal orientation. *See* Vertical/
    horizontal orientation
Horizontal space, usage, 90
Horizontal spacing, haphazardness, 91f
Horton, William, 53, 65
Housekeeping, usage, 152
HTML. *See* Hypertext Markup Language
Hue, impact, 76
Human requirements, 35–38
Human resources, 35–38. *See also* Portfolio
    site; Website owners
  availability, 2
Human-computer interaction, 12
Hype, avoidance, 11, 125. *See also* Marketing
  hype
Hypertext Markup Language (HTML), 5,
  121
  document, 119
  text, 123
  version, 122
Hypothesis (confirmation), qualitative
  research (usage). *See* User goals

I
IA. *See* Information architecture
Ideas, attention, 104
Identification capability, 120
iMac (Apple), 8
Images, 130
  cropping, 83f
  decisions, 82
  inclusion. *See* Informational images/
    graphics
  links, usage, 121
  portrayal, 117
  rotation, 83f
  sources, 81
iMovie, 162
Incentives, preparation, 151
Informality, 126

Information. *See* Navigation
  attention, 9, 120
  availability, 70
  chunks, 107
  context, display, 9, 68
  design, 129–130
    decisions, 61
  enhancement, 117–118
  gathering. *See* Content
  highlighting, 114–115
  memory, enhancement, 120
  objects, usage. *See* Card sorting
  organization, 51–53, 70
    approaches, 108
  placement. *See* Homepages
  presentation, 70
  spaces, impact, 91
  summarization, 120
  users
    attention, focus, 68
    guidance, 68
Information architects
  discussion, 125
  visual vocabulary (Garrett), 55
Information architecture (IA), 5, 17, 64
  conclusion, 60–61
  creation, 50–58
  decisions, 53
Informational images/graphics, inclusion,
    117, 120
Informed consent, 150–151
  form, 150–151
Input fields, 60
Interactivity
  persuasiveness, 123
  usage, 117, 123–124
International Organization for Standardiza-
    tion (ISO) 9241, 133–134
International users, 106
Interview. *See* Subject-Matter Experts
  findings, 33
Intrinsic metadata, 125
Introductory blurbs. *See* Portfolio
Introductory pages. *See* Flash
ISO. *See* International Organization for
    Standardization
Italics, usage (avoidance), 87
Items, categorization, 108
Iterative usability test, 139

J
Jargon, usage, 136
Java, 36

JavaScript, 118
Job descriptions, personas (relationship),
    43–44
Job-related experience, 148

K
Kilian Crawford, 109–110, 125, 130
Known-item search, impact, 159
Kostelnick, Charles, 100
Krug, Steve, 166

L
Landauer, Thomas K., 166
Language-related experience, 148
LATCH. *See* Location Alphabet Time
    Category Hierarchy
Layout, 88–93. *See also* Pages
  balance, 75
  consistency, 9
  design, grid (usage), 88–90
  elements, 96
  unity, 75
Leifer, Loring, 51, 65
Letter-size paper, size consideration, 88
Life goals, 45
Line length (reduced size), usage, 87
Linear sequences, 53
Links. *See* Cross-reference links; Websites
  adding, 115, 117–118
  embedding, 80
  inclusion, 126
  information enhancement, example, 118
  providing, 121
  usage, 86. *See also* Images
    strategies, 117–118
Lists, usage, 11, 86, 109, 112–113
Local secondary navigation, 63
Location Alphabet Time Category Hierarchy
    (LATCH), 51–52
Location-related experience, 148
Locker, Kitty, 106, 107, 130
Logical order, 107–108
Look/feel, defining. *See* Visual designs
Loranger, Hoa (profile), 62
Los Angeles County Art Museum, site
    homepage/content pages (example), 74f

M
Manipulation, avoidance, 125
Maps. *See* Portfolio site; Sites; Website
    maps
Marine, Larry, 47
  profile, 48–49

Market opportunity, size, 21–22
Market segmentation, 145
Marketing hype, avoidance, 110
Marketing-style language, usage (avoidance), 11
Mayer, Richard, 120, 130
Mayhew, Deborah J., 166
Mean (average), usage, 158
Memory, reinforcement, 104
Merritt, Susan, 66, 100
Message. *See* Nonverbal messages
  communication, 120
Metadata, 124. *See also* Administrative meta-
  data; Descriptive metadata; Intrinsic
  metadata
  types, 125
Mobile phone, 45
Moderator, effectiveness, 151–152
Moderator-driven approach, 142–143
Moderator-prompted/controlled test script, 143
Money, making (process), 21
Mood. *See* Websites
Morkes, John, 11, 18
Morville, Peter, 52, 54, 65, 80, 100
Mouseovers, visual appearance, 86
Moving, text, avoidance, 121
Mullet, Kevin, 69, 100
Multimedia, 98
  avoidance, 121
  consistency (style guide section), 96
  usage, 117, 120–123
Multiple-choice branches, 55

N
Narrative order, 107–108
National Geographic, Pearl Harbor multimedia history (example), 122f
Navigation, 64, 96. *See also* Local secondary
  navigation; Noun-based navigation
  bars, 58, 136
    example, 58f
  information, 88
  planning, 57–58
Navigational elements, 70, 80
  placement/style, 80
Navigational structure, 94
Nielsen, Jakob, 11, 18, 100, 102, 166
  experiments, 125
  guidelines, 109–110, 126, 131
  profile, 138–139
  suggestions, 153
Nomenclature, 12

Nonscrolling window, 119
Nonverbal messages, 104
Norman, Donald, 54, 65
Noun-based navigation, 58

O
Objective observer, 162
Objects, location identification, 70
Obligations, 127
Observation, 32. *See also* Representative
  users
  categorization. *See* Usability
  room, usage, 149
One-sentence summary, writing, 112
One-way mirror, usage, 149
Online environment, utilization, 115–125
Online portfolio
  content items, 3–4
  creation, 2–4
Online text, legibility (suggestions), 87
Open-ended questions, 104
Organizational issues, 160
Orientation. *See* Website users

P
Pages. *See* Grouped pages; Homepages;
  Subpages; Websites
  avoidance. *See* Flash
  connections, 5, 50
  design, creation, 70
  elements, placement, 75–76
  examples. *See* Portfolio
  inputs/outputs, possibilities, 50
  layout, 92, 99
    elements, 96
  links, 5
  scanning, example, 116f
Paper prototypes
  creation, 16
  planning, 78
Paper prototyping, usage, 62
Parallel structure, usage, 114
Pared-down approach, usage, 26
Participants (subjects). *See* Usability test
  participants
  digital photo, 33
  payment, 150
Participation statement, 150
Paths. *See* Connections/paths
PDA. *See* Personal digital assistant
PDF. *See* Portable Document Format
Perception, impact, 70
Personal digital assistant (PDA), 45

Personalization, 37
Personas, 15, 41–46. *See also* Complementary
    persona; Primary persona; Secondary
    persona; Users
  creation, 132
    tips, 43–46
  defining, 41–46
  example, 44f
  goals, understanding, 44–46
  relationship. *See* Job descriptions
  representations. *See* Behavior patterns
  set, size constraint, 44
  type, 107
Photographs, 98
  copyright issues, 81
  fair use, 81
  inclusion
    checklist, 81
    decisions, 81
  public domain, 81
  version, 123
Pilot test. *See* Usability tests
Pixelation, 82
Pixels
  dimensions, 97
  impact, 90, 119
  measurements, 96
Placement, 82
Platforms, typefaces (equivalency), 85
Political factors, 160
Pop-up windows, visual appearance, 86
Portable Document Format (PDF)
  documents, 5
  files, 3
Portfolio
  content, effectiveness, 11–12
  effectiveness, 13f
  items, introductory blurbs, 17
  pages, examples, 10f
Portfolio site
  checklist, 16–18
  creation, 1
  human/technical resources, 3
  map, 6f
    creation, 5–6
  owner goals, 2–3
  predictions, 15–16
  user goals, 3
Portfolio website collection, guidelines, 2–3
PowerPoint
  presentation, 162
  usage, 53, 59, 60
Price, Jonathan, 131

Primary persona, 43
Principles, importance, 127
Problem-solving abilities, emphasis, 12
Problems
  prioritization, 158–159
  rating, severity, 158–159
Processes, visualization, 120
Product-based models, 160
Production specifications (style guide
    section), 97
Prototype
  access, 149
  creation, 16
Prototyping, usage. *See* Paper prototyping
Proximity, 73–77
  principles, 93
  usage, 75f
Public domain. *See* Photographs
Purple, impact, 77
Purpose, discussion, 11

Q
Qualitative research, usage. *See* User goals
Quality assurance (QA) phase, 160
Quality control, 18, 130, 165
Questionnaires, preparation, 149
Questions. *See* Closed-ended questions;
    Follow-up questions; Open-ended
    questions
  list, creation, 30

R
Ragged-right margins, usage. *See* Body text
Readers
  attention, 9. *See also* Elements
  orientation, 11
Reading
  encouragement. *See* Users
  process, understanding. *See* World Wide
    Web
  speeds, 110
    impact, 115
Recommendations. *See* Findings/recommen-
    dations
  creation, 159–160
Redish, Janice C., 39, 166
  profile, 28–29
Reeves, Byron, 131
Reference letters, 4
References, usage, 86
Registration, user benefits, 143
Regular-weight typeface, usage, 85
Reiman, Robert M., 65

Relational database, 56
Relationships
  communication, 74
  display, 72
  indication, 75–77
  visualization, 120
Release forms, preparation, 149
Remote-control cameras, usage, 149
Repeat offenders, identification, 158
Representative users
  observation, 29–31
  recruitment, 134
Requirements document, 19–20
Requirements gathering, 2, 19
  checklist, 37–38
  schedule, 15
Research, capture. *See* Users
Results, 161
  analysis/reporting, 165
  presentation. *See* Usability
Résumé, PDF version, 4
Revenue goals, identification, 22–23
Reverse type, usage, 86
Reviews. *See* Expert reviews
Ries, Al, 25, 39
Roam, Dan, 8
Roberts, David D., 100
Rosenfeld, Louis, 52, 54, 65, 80, 100
Rubin, Jeffrey, 133–134, 159, 166
  profile, 135–136
Ruby (visual programming platform), 42
Run-through, 152

S
Sano, Darrell, 69, 100
Sans-serif typeface, usage, 87
Satisfaction, definition, 134
Saturation. *See* Color
  impact, 76
Scalability requirements. *See* Websites
Scan converter, usage, 149
Scannability, 129
Scenario-focused method, disadvantage, 143
Schedule, setup. *See* Usability test partici-
    pants
Schriver, Karen, 87, 90–91, 100, 131, 166
Screen sizes, 90
Screener
  example, 146–148
  writing, 145
Script, writing. *See* Usability test script
Scroll line, 119
Scrolling
  area, creation, 119

  usage, 115, 118–119
  window, 119. *See also* Nonscrolling
    window
Search capability, need. *See* Users
Search engine list, usage, 112
Secondary navigation. *See* Local secondary
    navigation
Secondary persona, 43
Security requirements. *See* Websites
SeeSpace, 32
Shaded background, adding, 86
Shared beliefs, 97
Shared language, 97
Sherman, Thomas (profile), 71–72
Sidebars, usage. *See* Summaries
Similarity, 73–74
  principles, 93
Simplicity, 69
Simplified usability test methods, usage,
    137
Sites. *See* Websites
  maps, 57
    example, 54f. *See also* Amazon.com
    variation, 58
Sizes, standardization/repetition, 9
Sizing, 82
SMEs. *See* Subject-Matter Experts
Specificity. *See* Usability test tasks
Spool, Jared M., 149, 166
Storyboards, usage, 122
Streaming media, 36
  implementation, excess, 121
Structure, consistency, 121
Style guide, 99
  usage, 128. *See also* Design
Style sheet, 69
  usage, 128
Subheadings, usage, 11, 109, 113–114
Subject-Matter Experts (SMEs), 103
Subject-Matter Experts (SMEs), interview,
    104
  conducting, 104
  post-interview phase, 104
  preparation, 104
Subjects. *See* Participants
Subpages, 5
Success
  measurement process, 22–23
  rate, 133
    recording, 156–157
Sume, David, 51, 65
Summaries. *See* Executive summary;
    Findings/recommendations
  sidebars, usage, 88

usage, 11, 109. *See also* Content
writing. *See* One-sentence summary
Symmetry
    diagonal axis, 93f
    usage, 92–93

T
Tables, usage, 86
Task flows, 40, 47, 63–64
    creation, 47, 132
    detail, example, 46f
    example, 45f
Task performance, 70
Task-oriented categories, 108
Task-oriented conceptualization. *See*
    Categories
Task-success numbers, assembling, 156–157
Team member, effectiveness, 16
Technical characteristics. *See* Color
Technical communication, 103
Technical limitations, design team
    (awareness), 34
Technical requirements, 35–38
    gathering, questions, 36
Technical resources, 35–38. *See also* Portfolio
    site
    availability, 2
Technical team, insider observations, 34
Technology
    assets, identification, 36
    backlash, 121
    planning, influence, 34
Tests. *See* Usability tests
Text. *See* Greeked text
    avoidance. *See* Blinking text; Moving
        text
    blank space, usage, 87
    blocks, 50
    capital letters, avoidance, 87
    concision, 11, 109, 110
        example, 110–112
    design, suggestions, 86–87
    equivalents, providing, 121
    explanation, 120
    focus, 11, 109, 110
    legibility, suggestions. *See* Online text
    visual design, 85–86
Textual content, creation, 132
Thank you notes, sending, 104
Think aloud
    participants, 140
    protocol, 153
Time stamp, usage, 162
Titles/headings, usage, 86

Tone, 129. *See also* Websites
    (style guide section), 96
Toor, Marcelle Lapow, 100
Topical categories, 108
Topical conceptualization. *See* Categories
Trends, visualization, 120
Trout, Jack, 25, 39
Trust, degree, 127
Type size, usage, 87. *See also* Print documents
Type usage. *See* Reverse type
Typefaces, 85
    equivalency. *See* Platforms
    usage. *See* Regular-weight typeface;
        Sans-serif typeface
Typography, 85–86, 98–99

U
UAT. *See* User acceptance testing
UIE. *See* User Interface Engineering
Unethical behavior, 127
Unity. *See* Layout
Upside-down L, 8, 58
Usability. *See* Discount usability
    (style guide section), 97
    analysis, 132
        checklist, 163–165
    definition, 133–136
    evaluations. *See* Heuristic usability
        evaluations
    findings, reporting, 134
    issues, 62
    observations, categorization, 158–159
    principles, 137
    problems, evaluation, 134
    results, presentation, 160–163
Usability test participants
    characteristics, 145, 148
    debriefing, 155
    incentives, preparation, 151
    list, 161
    personal characteristics, 148
    recruitment, 139, 145, 164
    schedule, setup, 151
    selection, 139, 145
    test location, knowledge, 151
Usability test scripts. *See* Exploratory test
    scripts; Feature-focused test scripts;
    Moderator-prompted/controlled test
    script; User-focused test scripts
    example, 141–142
    goals, matching. *See* Usability tests
    testing, 144
    types, 140
    writing, 140–142

Usability test tasks
  closure, 145
  concreteness, 144
  list, 161
  recording time, 158
  representation, 144
  simplicity, 145
  specificity, 144
Usability testing, 2, 12–14, 49
  data, transformation, 14
  environment, setup, 14, 139, 149–151
  labs, 135
  materials, preparation, 14
  participants, selection/recruitment, 14
  performing, 128
  process, 12–14, 139–160
  schedule, 16
Usability tests, 132. *See also* Benchmark
    usability test; Iterative usability
    test
  conducting, 14, 137, 139, 151–155, 164
  configuration, example. *See* Conference
    room usability test configuration
  data
    capture, 154–155, 164–165
    transformation, 139, 155–160
  definition, 133–137
  dress rehearsal, 144–145
  heuristic evaluations, contrast, 134–135
  initiation, tips, 153
  materials, preparation, 139, 149–151
  methodology/circumstances, description,
    160
  methods, usage. *See* Simplified usability
    test methods
  pilot test, 144–145
    conducting, 164
  plan, development, 12, 14, 139,
    140–145
  planning, 163–164
  procedure, 152–154
  results, example, 161f
  usability test script goals (matching), 145
  video capture, 154
USATODAY.com, WSJ.com (design
    differences), 68f
User acceptance testing (UAT), 160
User goals, 20, 26–35, 38
  accommodation, 27
  findings, debriefing/capturing, 33
  hypothesis (confirmation), qualitative
    research (usage), 35
  research, 31
    questions, 31

User Interface Engineering (UIE), 149
User-centered content labels, 80
User-directed data gathering, 33
User-focused chunks, content (breaking),
    107–108
User-focused content, maintenance,
    103–108
User-focused test scripts, 140, 143–144
Users. *See* International users
  attention, 68
    focus. *See* Information
  behaviors, impact. *See* Website owners
  benefits. *See* Registration
  data, understanding, 40–48
  experience, design, 6
    schedule, 15–16
  focus, 16–17, 125–126, 129
  guidance. *See* Information; Websites
  observation. *See* Representative users
  orientation. *See* Website users
  personas, 40, 63
  reading, encouragement, 68
  recruitment. *See* Representative users
  relationship, building, 106–107
  research, capture, 15
  search capability, need, 34
  tasks, performing. *See* Website users
  tasks, research, 31
    questions, 31

V
Value, impact, 76
Verbs, usage, 11, 109, 112
  example, 113
Vertical space, usage, 90
Vertical/horizontal orientation, 82
Vicarious experience, 162
Video capture. *See* Usability tests
Video editing, ethics, 162–163
Video files, 96
Video recording, usage, 150. *See also* Digital
    video recording
Video summary. *See* Findings/recommenda-
    tions
Video-editing software, 162
Videotaping/videotapes, watching, 156,
    157
Violet, impact, 77
Virtual reality tour. *See* 360-degree virtual-
    reality tour
Visio, usage, 53, 59, 60
Visual balance, maintenance, 92–93
Visual designs, 5, 8–10, 17, 57
  beginning, 60–61

checklist, 98–99
creation, 132
drafts, 73
elements, 66
look/feel, defining, 67–69
style guide section, 97
tools, 49–50
usage, 61–62
Visual direction, 79f
Visual dominance, 93
Visual drama, adding. *See* Websites
Visual elements, 9
Visual emphasis, 109
    providing, 120
Visual grouping (Gestalt principles), 72–79
Visual hierarchy, 79f
Visual patterns, creation, 107
Visual programming platform. *See* Ruby
Visual structure. *See* Content

W
Web-related experience, 148
Website maps, 4–5, 49, 64
    building, 53–56
    creation, 50–58, 132
Website owner brand
    benefit, 25–26
    positioning, 20, 23–26, 38
    tone/image. *See* Audience
Website owners
    audience, identification, 24
    branding goals, identification/analysis,
        15
    business goals, 20–23, 37–38
        identification/analysis, 15
        support, user behaviors (impact),
        23
    customers, identification, 24
    goals, 2
    human/technical resources/
        limitations, 20
    needs, identification/analysis, 15
    support, 36
Website users
    analysis, 15
    experience, 117
    goals, 20
    guidance, 68, 72
    observation, 134
    orientation, 112
    tasks, performing, 134
Websites
    architecture, 80
        creation, 16

audience
    defining, 9, 68
    goals/needs, 2
competition, identification, 22
content, user guidance, 9
creators, clarity, 125
design process, 2–4
designers, 20
functionality, finding, 9, 68
goals, clarity, 125
host, identification, 36
impact, increase, 9, 68
links, 4, 112
mood, 9, 68
outcomes, 21
ownership, cost, 36
pages, 50
    design/review, 149
processes, 50
prototype, 132
purpose/structure, 95f
scalability requirements, 36
security requirements, 36
structures, 53
text, concision, 110
tone, 9, 68
topic, linkage, 53
visual drama, adding, 120
Wilson, Catherine (profile), 105–106
Window sizes, consideration, 90
Wireframes, 5–8, 57
    checklist, 64
    creation, 132. *See also* Homepages
    example, 59f
    hand-drawn example, 7f
    initiation, 59–60
    preparation, example, 60f
    tools, 49–50
    usage, 58–61
Wireless microphones, usage, 149
Wish lists, 103
Word processor, 45
World Wide Web (Web)
    browser, 69
    checklist, 129–130
    content creation, 101
    experience, 33
    reading process, understanding,
        102
    wordiness, avoidance, 112
Writing samples, 3
WSJ.com, design differences. *See* USATO-
        DAY.com
Wurman, Richard Saul, 51, 65

X
XML, 36
  usage, 37

Y
Yahoo!
  approach, 55
  homepage, example, 56f

Yahoo!, goals, 54
Yellow, impact, 77
You Attitude, 106
    maintenance, 107

Credits

Page 4: From BBC website. William Philpott/Reuters; AP Photo/Wolfgang Schuessel; BBC News; BBC Video. **Figure 1.4, page 10:** Reprinted by kind permission of Jacqueline Jones Design. Reproduced by kind permission of Don Barnett, Nekton Inc. © Don Barnett, *www.donbarnett. com.* **Figure 1.5, page 13:** Reprinted by permission of Stuart Moulthrop, *http://iat.edu/ moulthrop.* **Figure 2.1, page 27:** Reprinted by permission of *The Wall Street Journal.* Copyright © 2003 Dow Jones & Company, Inc. All rights reserved worldwide. Copyright December 3, 2002. Reprinted with permission from USA TODAY. AP Photo/Charles Krupa; Disney Enterprises, Inc.; AP Photo, Disney Enterprises, Inc. and Nippy, Inc.; Fox Family Channel; Jim Ruymen/Reuters. **Figure 2.2, page 34:** Author's photo. **Page 49:** From BBC website. William Philpott/Reuters; AP Photo/Wolfgang Schuessel; BBC News; BBC Video. **Figure 3.6, page 56:** Reproduced with permission of Yahoo! Inc. © 2003 by Yahoo! Inc. YAHOO! and the YAHOO! logo are trademarks of Yahoo! Inc. **Figure 3.7, page 56:** Reproduced with permission of Google. **Figure 3.12, page 61:** © 2002 Amazon.com, Inc. All rights reserved. Reprinted by permission. **Figure 4.1, page 67:** Courtesy of Dell, Inc. Copyright © 2003 Dell Inc. All rights reserved. Reprinted by permission. **Figure 4.2, page 68:** Reprinted by permission of *The Wall Street Journal.* Copyright © 2003 Dow Jones & Company, Inc. All rights reserved worldwide. Copyright December 3, 2002. Reprinted with permission from USA TODAY. AP Photo/Charles Krupa; Disney Enterprises, Inc.; AP Photo, Disney Enterprises, Inc. and Nippy, Inc.; Fox Family Channel; Jim Ruymen/Reuters. **Figure 4.5, page 75:** From BBC website. AP Photo; AP Photo; Reuters; Council of Europe; BBC Video. **Figure 4.7, page 79:** Reprinted by kind permission of Jacqueline Jones Design. **Figure 4.9, page 83:** Author's photos. **Figure 4.10, page 84:** Website copyright Getty Images. Images copyright Stephen Sticker/Getty Images; Catherine Ledner/Getty Images; Don Bishop/Getty Images; Antonio Mo/Getty Images; Bobby Medel/National Geographic Society Image Collection. Reproduced by permission. **Figure 4.11, page 89:** From BBC website. AP Photo/Tomas Van Houtryve; BBC Video; AP Photo; AP Photo/Ali Fraidoon; AP Photo/INA. **Figure 4.16, page 95:** © Apple Computer, Inc. Used with permission. All rights reserved. Apple® and the Apple logo are registered trademarks of Apple Computer, Inc. Courtesy, Apple Computers and Jeremiah Cohick. Reproduced by permission of IBM. IBM Corporation; AP Photo/Chris O'Meara; Reuters. Copyright © 2002 The Economist Newspaper Ltd. All rights reserved. Reprinted with permission. Further reproduction prohibited. *www.economist.com.* **Figure 5.1, page 109:** Courtesy of Dell, Inc. All rights reserved. Reprinted by permission. **Figure 5.2, page 116:** The Motley Food, *www.fool.com.* Copyright © 2003 The Motley Fool, Inc. All rights reserved. Reproduced by permission. **Figure 5.4, page 123:** Second Story Interactive Studios © 2001 National Geographic Society